'Like Bach's great "Wachet auf" chorale, this walk through the weeks of Advent is both a carefully constructed meditation and an unsettling call to action. In the face of climate catastrophe, Nicholas Holtam invites us to pause in front of paintings that challenge us with the scale of our responsibilities, and reveal the grace we are promised if we tackle them. Poetry and music, painting and personal recollections combine in a new version of the Advent call to change our lives – while we still can. In Bach's words: Wake up!'
Neil MacGregor, broadcaster and former museum director

'We need a strong spirituality to help us address the issues of climate change. This Advent, Bishop Holtam invites the reader to an internal journey of self-discovery, where we recognize both our miraculous uniqueness and our inextricable unity with the rest of creation.'
Christiana Figueres, Head of the UN Climate Change Convention, 2010–2016

'The ideal Advent companion! Rooted in both the Bible and the current environmental crisis, Bishop Holtam's meditations help us to face the challenge of the Saviour who will finally come in judgement of what we have done to God's world, while we are preparing to offer all we have to the Babe of Bethlehem. Read it yourself daily, study it in weekly groups – but, most importantly, wake from sleep and act now before it is too late.'
The Revd Canon Professor Richard A. Burridge, biblical scholar and Canon Theologian

Nicholas Holtam was a Durham geographer before training for ordination at King's College London, and Westcott House, Cambridge. After a curacy in Stepney, he taught ethics and mission at Lincoln Theological College before becoming Vicar of the Isle of Dogs in London's Docklands and Vicar of St Martin-in-the-Fields, Trafalgar Square. He was Bishop of Salisbury from 2011 to 2021 and the Church of England's lead bishop on the environment, chairing the Environmental Working Group from 2014 to 2021. He led prayers and spoke regularly in the House of Lords and contributed to international conferences as well as doing all the day-to-day stuff with clergy and people that occupy and sometimes delight a bishop in the Diocese of Salisbury. His previous books are *A Room with a View: Ministry with the World at Your Door* (SPCK, 2008) and *The Art of Worship: Paintings, Prayers and Readings for Meditation* (National Gallery, 2011). He lives in Brighton and is married to Helen who is a Quaker. They have four adult children and a growing number of grandchildren.

SLEEPERS WAKE

Getting serious about climate change

The Archbishop of York's Advent Book 2022

Nicholas Holtam

First published in Great Britain in 2022

Society for Promoting Christian Knowledge
36 Causton Street
London SW1P 4ST
www.spck.org.uk

British Library Cataloguing-in-Publication Data
A catalogue record for this book is available from the British Library

ISBN 978–0–281–08684–9
eBook ISBN 978–0–281–08685–6

1 3 5 7 9 10 8 6 4 2

Typeset by Fakenham Prepress Solutions, Fakenham, Norfolk NR21 8NL
Printed and bound in Turkey by Mega Print

eBook by Fakenham Prepress Solutions, Fakenham, Norfolk NR21 8NL

Produced on paper from sustainable sources

For the grandchildren

'Sleepers, wake!' the watch-cry pealeth,
While slumber deep each eyelid sealeth:
Awake, Jerusalem, awake!
Midnight's solemn hour is tolling,
And seraph-notes are onward rolling;
They call on us our part to take.
Come forth, ye virgins wise:
The Bridegroom comes, arise!
Alleluia!
Each lamp be bright
With ready light
To grace the marriage feast tonight.
(P. Nicolai, 1556–1608; tr. Frances E. Cox, 1812–97)

Contents

Contents

Illustrations

Foreword

The urgency of life surrounds us – changing weather patterns are dramatically affecting the way we live and our reliance upon the earth in its abundance is something we can no longer take for granted. We are tasked with caring for God's creation in its entirety – the soil, the water sources, the animals, the biodiversity, the plants, the atmosphere and of course God's people – and this task is now more urgent and more challenging than it has ever been. So this book is timely, asking us to act out our faith in relation to care for the earth, but also drawing upon the author's expertise and many years of experience in climate justice.

As Bishop of Salisbury, Nick Holtam was the Church of England's lead bishop on environmental concerns. In the Church itself, in the House of Lords, and in teaching and preaching in the community, Nick is someone who has helped to develop an overdue Christian response to the climate emergency that our world faces. I am delighted that he has written this book. In it he interweaves theology, politics, poetry and art. He asks us to respond, to heed the call to be stewards of God's creation.

Advent is a time of preparation, a time of expectation, a time of waiting. And yet, with regard to the climate crisis, we can wait no more. If we expect at the very least to stop our destruction of the earth, never mind to reverse the damage we have caused, we need to be prepared drastically to alter the way we live. Nick Holtam invites us to journey this Advent not only to the manger, but to the hope of God's kingdom come on earth, a hope that preserves, sustains and nurtures all life.

Advent is also a time of discomfort – the Christ child is not the happy, rosy-cheeked baby, the manger is not the cosy retreat depicted on our Christmas cards. Emmanuel, God with us, is the shock of God's presence in this world, calling us to wake up, to focus on what is important, to do justice and to love kindness.

Sleepers Wake confronts us with the harsh realities of the climate crisis, offering bite-sized chunks that we can process throughout Advent. The message, however, is not one of doom, for this book is shot through with hope. Scripture and practical suggestions intersperse the prophetic message of the reality of what our action, and inaction, is doing to the world. The examples of saints ask us how we are responding in terms of prayer and a communal rule of life. These are held up as an inspiration for us to live as God's stewards in the world.

You are, therefore, about to embark on a challenging read. But you are also invited to participate through prayer and action in the change that will mean a flourishing life for the whole cosmos. There is surely no more beautiful message for Advent than this!

Stephen Cottrell
Archbishop of York

Acknowledgements

Thanks to my former colleagues and to friends who helped when the writing got difficult, especially Annette Atkins, James Woodward and Richard Burridge.

And thanks to Alison Barr of SPCK, patient and helpful beyond measure, and to Rachel Ashley-Pain who did the detail enjoyably.

Introduction

Advent is urgent. We are getting ready for Christmas and there is a lot to do. We are also reminding ourselves that Christ will come again. We do not know when that will be so we need to be prepared. Most of the time we just get on with life and live without much urgency, but that feels less possible in a world that is becoming more and more alarmed by the climate and environmental crises.

The care of creation is also urgent but it is not a new priority for Christians. The Scriptures delight in the gift of creation; they contain laws about living sustainably on the land, not taking more than our fair share, and what it means to love our neighbours – including the stranger. What *is* new is that we are having to respond to a problem of our own making, caused by those who have not lived with reverence.

Over the past few decades, a theological consensus has grown among the Orthodox Church, the Roman Catholic Church and the World Council of Churches that this crisis must be addressed urgently. In the 1980s, the Anglican Church worldwide developed what are known as the Five Marks of Mission:

1 To proclaim the good news of the kingdom.
2 To teach, baptize and nurture new believers.
3 To respond to human need by loving service.
4 To transform unjust structures of society, to challenge violence of every kind and pursue peace and reconciliation.
5 To strive to safeguard the integrity of creation, and sustain and renew the life of the earth.

The fifth mark was added because, without it, the first four did not make adequate sense of what it means to live as a Christian in today's world. For the Church of England, our ecumenical partners and the Anglican Communion, this fifth mark has become a greater priority as the sense of an environmental crisis has deepened.

The major Church of England report on the environment, 'Sharing God's Planet' (2005), led to the creation of the Church of England's national environmental campaign, Shrinking the Footprint, and a further Mission and Public Affairs Council report, 'Climate Change and Human Security', in 2008. Also in 2008, the Ethical Investment Advisory Group (EIAG), which advises the Church of England's National Investing Bodies, published a new policy on climate change. However, in the light of the rapidly changing and developing crisis, in 2011 they were asked to undertake a much deeper theological review, with detailed practical proposals for the way to a greener, carbon-neutral future. This was completed during 2014, and remains the undergirding theological and biblical assessment, while its practical recommendations for investment are updated regularly.[1]

In 2014, following the General Synod's agreement to a motion that came from Southwark Diocese reaffirming its desire to play a leading role in the effort to prevent dangerous climate change, the Archbishops of Canterbury and York asked me to lead on the environment and chair a new Environmental Working Group (EWG). The members of the EWG, and the small staff supporting us, have been magnificent in their commitment and expertise. I cannot thank them enough, nor the diocesan environmental officers, many of whom are volunteers, nor the generous collaborators from outside the EWG, who have helped ensure that the fifth mark of mission is integral to the Church of England.

The scale of the problem is such that what has been achieved by the Church can only be regarded as modest, because it is nothing like enough to save the planet. However, it has been inspiring to see how care for the environment has grown locally and nationally throughout the Church of England in this time and place. In 2020, General Synod became ever more ambitious for us as a church to be net zero by 2030, as part of the global effort to decarbonize by 2050. This is a huge task. Every diocese has an environmental officer, working with churches, chaplaincies, schools, institutions and individuals who have made it a priority to care for the environment.

Among the bishops, I inherited great work done by Richard Chartres (London) and James Jones (Liverpool). At the annual residential meeting of bishops there was a fringe meeting, which was not part of the main agenda.

This 'environmental breakfast' was attended by about a fifth of all the Church of England's bishops, some of whom had a high level of interest and expertise. Following the General Synod motion in 2014, all bishops made the care of God's creation one of their priorities and the number attending the environmental breakfast grew rapidly. At the last meeting before the pandemic, over two-thirds came. During the pandemic we held a similar meeting online and 70 bishops met for tea with Christiana Figueres, formerly Executive Secretary of the UN Framework Convention on Climate Change, and Nigel Topping, the UK's High Level Climate Action Champion for the UN Climate Change summit in Glasgow. I am grateful for the ways in which my episcopal colleagues have engaged with the task.

I am also grateful that the Archbishop of York suggested, when I retired as Bishop of Salisbury in July 2021 and the role of lead bishop for the environment passed to the Bishop of Norwich, that I should write this Advent Book as a way of trying to distil what I had learned. It has been an unusually challenging book to write, partly because of the transition in my own life into 'retirement', partly because I have no neat distillation of my learning, and partly because there has been so much disturbing news on climate change and the environment. In the final weeks of writing, the Intergovernmental Panel on Climate Change (IPCC) published its latest analysis of the dangers of climate change and the need for a more urgent response. The upsurge in energy prices was compounded by the massive impact on supply following the Russian invasion of Ukraine. This inevitably created political pressure for the UK to expand oil and gas production as well as renewables. A UK Energy Strategy was published, heavily dependent on new nuclear and offshore wind, but lacking commitment to onshore wind (the cheapest and quickest source of electricity), and the government shows little interest in home insulation, which would be the most effective domestic energy-saving measure. Politicians mostly talk well when it comes to the environment, but there's often a gap between words and action, and a series of reports has drawn attention to the widening disparity between targets and delivery. In this book I have tried to focus on giving information, applying theology and uncovering and developing spirituality, but like it or not, there is a political aspect to the care of the environment.

Perhaps my greatest anxiety as lead bishop related to this: agreeing the strategic direction of travel is relatively easy (although agreeing the aim to be net zero by 2030 involved heated discussion), but it is much more difficult to agree the means and pace of our travelling together. It is a long journey. Our different experiences and insights can cause us to fall out with one another and waste time and energy in disagreement over tactics. We can lose trust, rather as the Israelites did with their murmurings in the wilderness. It took Moses 40 years to lead them from slavery to the freedom of the promised land. We do not have that long. The Church is a microcosm of the wider world and, as we all need one another and must journey together, it has something to offer what can be a fractious environmental movement.

General Synod called for the development of 'eco theology' and the EWG put some effort into encouraging and developing this. It was being developed anyway and some marvellous books have been written and outstanding work done, both locally and nationally. I learned we did not need new theology so much as to rediscover the wisdom of Christianity in caring for the earth and to apply this to our context. Uncovering some of the old ways in the Church's life is helping us today.

The stand-out achievements for the Church of England in the past decade have been, first, the development of 'Eco Church' by the Christian environmental charity A Rocha – of which so many churches have made good use – and second, the response of those who oversee the Church's financial investments to Synod's call for alignment with the environmental mission and purpose of the Church. Christiana Figueres said to the bishops that the Church of England has given leadership in this area. The team leading on investments and the Church Commissioners under the leadership of Loretta Minghella, then First Estates Commissioner, have been outstanding. It is good to have something done by the Church of England that is so widely perceived to be world class.

'Sleepers, Wake' is a hymn many of us will sing this Advent to the setting of a Bach chorale. As we approach midwinter and prepare for Christmas, Advent calls us to wake up, pay attention, stay sober and be alert to God and to what is happening in the world around us. The behaviour of human beings is the major current cause of climate change, and has the potential to become the sixth major event to result in the mass extinction of life on planet earth. We know this, yet we are still in danger of sleepwalking towards catastrophe.

The world around us celebrates Christmas throughout Advent, though many families and schools feel that the season is something of a pressure.

So do many retail businesses, an astonishing number of which make most of their year's profits in the weeks leading up to Christmas. However, for all the busyness we have created, the season of Advent into Christmas remains full of charm and beauty as we celebrate the birth of a baby – God with us – in Bethlehem more than 2,000 years ago. Yet this is not just a story of long ago and far away. It continues in the present and points to the future. We are being awakened to Christ's second coming and the completion of his work on earth. We are being called to live as citizens of God's kingdom in the here and now. It's what we pray for in the Lord's Prayer, 'Thy kingdom come on earth as it is in heaven', and it's what Christians pin their hopes on.

The language, imagery and stories of Advent are load-bearing and hopeful in the ways they shape our understanding, choices and actions. As Bishop of Salisbury, I found it striking that the biggest services of the cathedral's year were the 'Darkness to Light' ones at the beginning of Advent. People came in their thousands (before the pandemic, at least), so we held three services on successive nights over the Advent Sunday weekend. In a packed cathedral, we waited in the still, dark silence for the procession of music and Bible readings to unfold, and for 1,400 candles to be lit in celebration of the glory of the Advent hope that God comes among us in Jesus Christ – again and again and again. In this context, the Church can face with deep confidence the complex realities of life and death.

We can't help but be aware that we face some very complex realities in the present time, including the impact of the pandemic and its economic and social consequences. The silence and beauty of the first spring in lockdown, when the streets and skies were empty, were a poignant reminder of the slower and longer-term implications of climate change and environmental degradation. We are sensing an opportunity to do things differently, and an Advent-like urgency is needed in making our response.

Many Christians concerned about climate change and the environment were struck by something said by Gus Speth, an American environmental lawyer who co-founded the Natural Resources Defense Council and became Dean of the Yale School of Forestry and Environmental Studies:

I used to think the top environmental problems were biodiversity loss, eco system collapse and climate change. I thought that with 30 years of good science we could address those problems. But I was wrong. The top environmental problems are selfishness, greed and apathy – and to deal with those we need a spiritual and cultural transformation – and we scientists don't know how to do that.[2]

Spirituality is the integration of our beliefs, values and actions. It draws on the wisdom accumulated in a religion and culture. Christian spirituality is shaped in the Church by Scripture, tradition and reason, and is made active through thought and prayer. Spirituality is at the heart of individuals and communities. It motivates us, addresses questions of what we truly want for ourselves and for one another, and holds us to account. Given that 80 per cent of the world's population have a religious identity, faith and spirituality are important resources to mobilize people in response to climate change and the care of God's creation.

Perhaps it is because of what I have learned and been most influenced by in the past eight years that this is a book about Christian spirituality for Advent in the context of the climate and environmental crises. It is a more personal volume than I expected at the outset and one that draws on my experience of ordained ministry over more than 40 years. The structure is as follows: the first verse of the hymn 'Sleepers, Wake' gives a framework for the four weeks of Advent, and daily reflections explore how Christianity resources us to get serious about the care of God's creation. It is a challenging book. Political, ecclesiastical and personal issues arise throughout. You might want to read it individually or as part of a group. There are a few focused questions at the end of each week and a suggestion that the first question should always be 'What struck you?', simply because when a group starts with that, I am usually surprised by what I missed but others noticed! It is for you to turn what is given into prayer and action. At the end is a short list of websites and books I have found useful, to help you take things further.

To strive to safeguard the integrity of creation and sustain and renew the life of the earth is integral to being a Christian today. We are making progress, but there are only 27 years to 2050, when the world has committed to be net zero. For all of us, the Archbishop of York's Advent Book is an urgent call to action. Sleepers, wake!

Almighty God,
give us grace to cast away the works of darkness

and to put on the armour of light,
now in the time of this mortal life,
in which your Son Jesus Christ came to us in great humility;
that on the last day,
when he shall come again in his glorious majesty
    to judge the living and the dead,
we may rise to the life immortal;
through him who is alive and reigns with you,
in the unity of the Holy Spirit,
one God, now and for ever. Amen.[3]

WEEK 1

'Sleepers, wake!' the watch-cry pealeth,
While slumber deep each eyelid sealeth:
Awake, Jerusalem, awake!

Advent Sunday

The writing is on the wall

Rembrandt's painting of Belshazzar's feast makes a dramatic start to our Advent. The writing is literally on the wall but the people in the room can't read it and don't understand what it means.

Rembrandt depicts a story told in the book of Daniel chapter 5 about the Judean exile in Babylon following the destruction of Jerusalem in 587 BC. The Babylonian king Belshazzar held a feast for a thousand of his lords, wives and concubines. When they were drunk, he commanded they use the sacred vessels from the temple that had been in Jerusalem. It was an offensive, deeply shocking, sacrilegious act. Rembrandt captures so well the desecration and the king's terror as the fingers of a human hand appeared and wrote on the wall. Belshazzar cried aloud for help from the wise men of Babylon. Whoever could read and interpret this writing would be clothed in purple, have a gold chain put around his neck and rank third in the kingdom. None of the wise men could read the writing.

The queen, however, knew of Daniel, one of the exiles, who was able to interpret dreams, explain riddles and solve problems. Daniel looked at the wall and saw the inscription, *Mene, Mene, Tekel and Parsin*, which meant that God had numbered the days of Belshazzar's kingdom and brought it to an end; Belshazzar had been weighed in the scales and found wanting. That night he was killed and Darius the Mede received the kingdom (Dan. 5.30–31).

For the Jews, the exile became a defining experience. Adversity turned out to be the seedbed of faith and new life. Through humiliation they learned to be faithful again. Though their exile began as a time of lament, looking back and remembering what they had lost – 'By the rivers of Babylon – there we sat down and there we wept when we remembered Zion' (Ps. 137.1) – God was at work in the world. They came to see that Israel's capture by the

Babylonians was God's punishment for their faithlessness. However, in exile their best interests were also the Babylonians' best interests, as is made clear in the letter written to them by the prophet Jeremiah, who was left back in Jerusalem: 'Seek the welfare of the city where I have sent you into exile, and pray to the LORD on its behalf, for in its welfare you will find your welfare' (Jer. 29.5–7).

Four centuries later, the story of Daniel and Belshazzar's feast was told to encourage the Jews who were then being persecuted after the second destruction of the Jerusalem temple. Its restoration is still celebrated by Jews today in the eight-day Festival of Lights, Hanukkah, which usually falls in Advent and in 2022 is from 18 to 26 December. There is repeated experience here.

Advent in the northern hemisphere occurs at the darkest time of the year. It is a season of judgement, which both reveals the truth and gives us an opportunity to respond. The truth is that we have not bestowed the care we should on God's gift of creation. We are misusing it, we lack reverence, we are complacent. Better care for God's creation will help us return to God. The pandemic and the subsequent economic crisis, climate change and the environmental destruction of our times have made us realize, once again, that we are in this together – and that no one is safe until everyone is safe.

Climate scientists say that the writing has been on the wall for 30 years, but policy makers are not responding quickly enough. Many see faith as a resource for facing reality and making change. They think we Christians could do more to sound the alarm and point out the connections between belief and action. They recognize that, around the world, faith communities have the potential for collective action.

Advent calls us to wake up and *live in the faith* that we are already citizens of the kingdom of heaven because Christ is our certain hope. It is a time of judgement *and* of opportunity. The writing is on the wall and in this first week of Advent we will seek to read it and understand its meaning, as the world wakes up to what is happening because of what we are doing. 'You know what time it is, how it is now the moment for you to wake from sleep. For salvation is nearer to us now than when we became believers; the night is far gone, the day is near' (Rom. 13.11–12).

Monday

Global warming

Human activity is causing climate change, there is no doubt about it. We live in the Anthropocene era, which means our era is defined by the substantial impact human beings are having on the planet. Our behaviour is defining what is happening to our world, and there is anxiety that we are hastening our extinction. However, because things appear to us to be moving relatively slowly, we have failed to react with sufficient speed. It might be helpful to think of 'boiled-frog syndrome', where the water heats so slowly that the frog does not move – until it's got so hot it cannot move (by which time it's too late).

The average global surface temperature between 2001 and 2020 was 1.0 °C higher than between 1850 and 1900. This may not seem much, but it is having major effects and we have been watching these intensify for decades: more extreme weather events, the ice cap and glaciers melting, sea level rising, wildfires, coral bleaching, flooding, desertification and so on. It is a global problem but it has been difficult for nations to make a concerted response.

Ban Ki-moon, then UN Secretary General, said the talks at the UN Climate Change conference in Paris in 2015 were the biggest and most complex of which he'd ever been part. They took place in the aftermath of acts of terrorism in which 130 people were killed and 416 injured. This made the 12,000 participants and the 48,000 others supporting the summit even more determined to get a good outcome.

The Paris Agreement was undoubtedly a breakthrough and nearly all the countries of the world signed up to:

- work towards being carbon neutral by the end of the century;
- commit to a long-term goal of keeping the increase in average temperature to well below 2 °C above pre-industrial levels;

The Big Church Read

Did you know that you can read

Sleepers Wake

as a Big Church Read?

Join together with friends, your small group
or your whole church, or do it on your own,
as Nicholas Holtam leads you through the book.

Visit **www.thebigchurchread.co.uk** or use the **QR code below
to watch exclusive videos from Nicholas Holtam**
as he explores the ideas and themes of *Sleepers Wake*.

**The Big Church Read will also provide you with a reading plan
and discussion questions** to help guide you through the book.

It's free to join in and a great way to read through
Sleepers Wake!

- aim to limit the increase to 1.5 °C since this would significantly reduce risks and the impact of climate change;
- recognize the need for global emissions to peak as soon as possible, and that this will take longer for developing countries;
- undertake rapid reductions thereafter in accordance with the best available science.

A variety of scenarios could play out, and we ought to pray and work for the best, but we are not yet close to being on track to limiting global warming to 'well below' 2 °C above pre-industrial levels, let alone cap warming at 1.5 °C. But at Paris, countries made themselves accountable to one another, ratcheting up their commitments year on year. In Paris, it looked as though we were heading for global warming of about 3.7 °C. After the Glasgow summit in November 2021, we might now be heading towards warming of between 2.7 °C and 3.2 °C, depending on the thoroughness with which nations act on the agreements. It is a major achievement *and it is nothing like enough*.

The difference between global warming of 1.5 °C and 2 °C would mean sea levels rising 10 cm more. The Arctic Ocean would be free of ice for 1 in 10 summers rather than 1 in 100, and 99 per cent of coral reefs would die rather than 60 to 70 per cent.[1] The impact on people would be huge, with more extreme weather including larger areas experiencing barely tolerable heat and spontaneous fires. There would be three times the rate of loss of species and twice the amount of thawing of Arctic permafrost, causing the release of greenhouse gases. The dangers of exceeding a 'tipping point' into exponential change are considerable.

Because the science is complex, most of us find it difficult to take in the numbers and understand the writing on the wall. Ed Hawkins, a professor at Reading University, developed 'warming stripes' as a way of showing complex data in a meaningful way for non-specialists. The stripes illustrate the average annual temperature increase of approximately 1.0 °C from 1850 to 2020 at Reading. Each of the 170 vertical stripes represents the average temperature for a single year, relative to the average temperature over the period as a whole. Shades of blue indicate cooler than average years, while shades of red show years that were hotter than average. The ten warmest years in the UK have all been recorded since 2002, with the hottest during this period being 2014. Globally, 2021 was the sixth warmest year on record.

It has been said that the warming stripes graphics are a bit like the colour field painting of the mid-twentieth-century abstract impressionists Mark Rothko, Clyfford Still and Barnett Newman. For them, what an image expresses is self-evident. Perhaps because the impacts of global warming are becoming more apparent, the warming stripes have caught people's imagination, and all around the world communities have been encouraged to *#show your stripes*. The stripes have become a symbol of the climate emergency. Red means danger.

During the pandemic, we have got used to politicians saying they are 'following the science'. They also need to follow the science in relation to climate change and global warming. The numbers are difficult for most of us to read and interpret, but at the beginning of Advent our first task is to wake up to what we are doing to the world God has given us. Facing the truth often feels challenging, but not facing the truth will be much worse.

This anonymous prayer opens us up to the truth of God:

From the arrogance that thinks it knows all truth;
From the laziness that is content with half-truth;
From the cowardice that shrinks from new truth,
O God of truth, deliver us. Amen.

Tuesday

The path to net zero

Our rapid consumption of fossil fuels that took millions of years to lay down in the earth is the main cause of global warming. The Industrial Revolution (powered by coal) brought enormous good to people. Thanks to our God-given creativity, we are more prosperous, enjoy better health and live longer than our predecessors. These benefits, however, have not been justly distributed, and the twentieth century saw a desire to advance economic development in a fairer fashion. There was an element of enlightened self-interest in this. The most prosperous will not be safe and secure when there are large numbers not profiting as they should from the world's development.

What has been beneficial is no longer so, or at least is no longer unambiguously so. We will be dependent on fossil fuels for some time to come, but we know our use of them is harming the world, and urgent action is needed to rapidly reduce the damage. The transition to a carbon neutral, net-zero economy is difficult. There are tensions between policy makers and environmental campaigners. On the whole, the policy makers are optimistic and encouraging as they work to maintain our confidence in the collective effort. Decarbonization is happening faster than many would have thought possible ten years ago. The campaigners, on the other hand, believe we've started too late and that change has to happen now and more quickly than is realistic. But how do we define 'realistic' when the way we're actually living compromises the future?

Change towards becoming carbon neutral has to be front-loaded to prevent the scale of the problem we are facing becoming even greater. Much is possible with existing technology, and ambition is growing. Christiana Figueres thinks there is unstoppable momentum towards a future of prosperity, growth and clean energy through climate leadership, market forces and the digital revolution. There is plenty of good news. For example, the Netherlands is committed to becoming a no-waste 'circular economy' by 2050. China is adding 9,500 electric buses – equivalent to London's entire fleet – every five weeks. In the UK, coal will not be used for generating electricity after October 2024. In the first three months of 2022, wind turbines generated record amounts of electricity – almost as much as that produced by gas-fired power stations. In the USA, 50 per cent of coal-fired power stations have closed. (The rate of closure didn't change even when President Trump was in office, but maybe that's an indication that change is happening but not fast enough.) We all need to be more intentional in the journey to net zero. The report published by the IPCC in April 2022 managed to be both urgent and encouraging. It stated that global carbon emissions continued to rise last year, and if we are to have any chance of limiting global warming to 1.5 degrees by 2050, peak carbon emissions must be reached by 2025 and reduced by 45 per cent by 2030.

In October 2021 the UK government published its strategy for getting to net zero through a ten point plan:

- advancing offshore wind
- driving the growth of low-carbon hydrogen
- delivering new and advanced nuclear power
- accelerating the shift to zero-emission vehicles
- green public transport, cycling and walking
- 'jet-zero' and green ships
- greener buildings
- investing in carbon capture, usage and storage
- protecting our natural environment
- green finance and innovation.

This is the UK's framework for a new industrial revolution to move our dependence on fossil fuels to sustainable sources of energy. The plan's assumptions about the timescale needed for the development of new technology are extremely optimistic. The high price of oil and gas has added pressure to change from these harmful sources, but low-carbon hydrogen, carbon-neutral aircraft and ships and the development of carbon capture and storage at scale will not come quickly. The absence of proposals to harness tidal power is surprising. It is technically challenging and initially expensive but has huge potential for the UK. Even when existing technology is all that is needed, experience suggests we have not always demonstrated the commitment required to deliver. For example, in 2016, energy standards were reduced because of the pressure to build more new homes and there has been a repeated failure to implement an effective plan to insulate old homes. In February 2022, our bills were estimated to be £2.5 billion higher as a direct result.

Nuclear energy is seen as the only realistic way of providing a reliable continuous supply of carbon-free electricity. The need for energy security and the increased cost of oil and gas have created greater pressure to move ahead with this quickly. The nuclear industry is confident about safety, but that assumes things remain relatively stable in terms of politics, economics and the environment, which may be optimistic. There have been serious accidents at Windscale (1957, Cumbria, UK), Kyshtym (1957, Russia), Three Mile Island (1979, Pennsylvania, USA), Chernobyl (1986, Ukraine, then in the Soviet Union) and Fukushima (2011, Japan). The handling and storage of radioactive waste is a long-term legacy. Although in the UK the main political parties have made a renewed commitment to nuclear energy, it is expensive and for good reasons has its opponents.

Extinction Rebellion (XR) is a movement that has protested at what is perceived to be a 'business as usual' approach that does not adequately address the scale of the climate emergency. The disruption caused by XR has not always been well targeted, has been widely perceived as irritating and is sometimes counter-productive. It is hard to see how gluing yourself to a train and disrupting public transport helps XR's cause. But like it or not, its activists have changed the debate and done an impressive job of raising the public's awareness, waking more of us up to the urgency of the climate and environmental crises.

In the last few years, many councils as well as parliaments across the UK have declared a climate emergency. Similarly (as is mentioned in the Introduction), in 2020 the General Synod of the Church of England recognized the climate emergency and committed the Church to be net zero by 2030. It is an impossibly ambitious target. However, those who proposed it did so in order to pick up the pace, and that is proving effective. Christians and churches are often key within their communities in highlighting issues and helping people address them in ways that inform and educate more widely.

Nearly 3,000 years ago, an Israelite prophet challenged his hearers in this way:

> He has told you, O mortal, what is good;
> and what does the LORD require of you
> but to do justice, and to love kindness,
> and to walk humbly with your God?
> (Mic. 6.8)

What does this mean for us today?

Wednesday

Biodiversity

Climate change is only one element of the environmental crisis. The dramatic loss of biodiversity is another big part of the problem arising from the failure to care for God's creation. Biodiversity is how we describe the variety of all living things on earth and how they fit together in the web of life. It provides many of our basic needs, including oxygen, water and food. A million animal and plant species are said to be threatened with extinction, though in truth it is difficult to count. New species are constantly being discovered and estimates about the proportion of species at risk vary. What is clear is that the pace of loss is increasing. The UK is one of the world's most nature-depleted countries, putting us in the bottom 10 per cent for biodiversity. So we are at risk – and we are contributing to our own destruction.

In October 2021, a month before the Glasgow COP26 on Climate Change, a virtual meeting began online – the fifteenth UN Biological Diversity summit – with the hope of meeting face to face in Kunming, China, in 2022. Transformative changes are needed to restore and protect nature. It is staggering that none of the 20 targets agreed for the UN's Decade of Biodiversity 2011–20 has been fully met, and only six have been 'partially achieved'. According to Sir Robert Watson, who chaired the Intergovernmental Science-Policy Platform on Biodiversity and Ecosystem Services (IPBES), the UN's scientific body on nature:

> The overwhelming evidence is that the health of ecosystems on which we and all other species depend is deteriorating more rapidly than ever. We are eroding the very foundations of our economies, livelihoods, food security, health and quality of life worldwide.[2]

Concern is often expressed about the impact of human overpopulation on the earth's biodiversity, and Roman Catholic teaching is sometimes criticized because it prohibits the use of artificial barriers to conception. However, if this is a problem, it cannot be the main one. The rise and fall of birth rates is due to multiple factors. For example, the poverty strongly associated with the world's highest birth rates in Central and West Africa suggests overpopulation will be most effectively addressed by greater economic prosperity. The world's more developed countries are now concerned about population decline, as in Japan, Taiwan, Portugal, South Korea and Greece. Our responsibility is to live more lightly on the earth, to be alert to how we are having an impact on its resources.

Most countries now have policies intended to address environmental degradation. In 2020, the UK Parliament passed an Environment Act with a 25-year aim of protecting and restoring the natural environment. The hope is that ours will be the first generation to leave the environment in a better state than we inherited it. The Act made provision for the setting of long-term environmental targets for air quality, water, biodiversity and resource efficiency and waste reduction, along with the production of statutory Environmental Improvement Plans. It lacked detail but it does set direction and provide for accountability. The task is to ensure that action matches intent and in this, the role of campaigning groups will be essential.

All of us can make the most of the opportunities we have to enhance biodiversity locally. As the bishop of a largely rural diocese, I undertook regular farm visits to see how agriculture was responding to the environmental challenges in relation to land use. On Wiltshire's Marlborough Downs, a group of farmers started to work together in 2012 to create a Nature Improvement Area. They have greatly enriched soil quality and restored flora and fauna so arable land now supports a diversity of wildlife. Rare arable plants survive in field margins, and stone curlews, skylarks, grey partridges, lapwings and corn buntings have returned in larger numbers.

Churchyards collectively across the country are the size of a national park. The gospel began at an empty tomb, and there is something profoundly satisfying about 'living churchyards', where an oasis of nature has been created in a place where the dead are buried so as to encourage greater life and biodiversity. Some churchyards are part of 'bee lines', providing routes for pollinators to thrive. County Wildlife Trusts have given invaluable support to churches, and Caring for God's Acre have an excellent website. Being imaginative about urban churchyards can also make a big difference to the way in which biodiversity is enhanced. Wherever they are, small groups of people working together to take action helps them not only to educate themselves and their community, but also to change the way we live in rural, suburban and urban settings.

We can run headlong into disaster, or we can sleepwalk into it, but we can no longer say that we do not know the impact of the way we are living. It is only in facing the reality that we can find the way forward. As John's Gospel puts it: 'Then Jesus said to the Jews who had believed in him, "If you continue in my word, you are truly my disciples; and you will know the truth, and the truth will make you free"' (John 8.31–32).

Thursday

Laudato si'

The most influential Christian contribution on the environment in recent years is Pope Francis's encyclical, a letter known by its opening words, *Laudato si'*. Pope Francis is quoting the beautiful canticle by St Francis of Assisi, 'On Care for Our Common Home':

> 'Praise be to you, my Lord, through our Sister, Mother Earth, who sustains and governs us, and who produces various fruit with coloured flowers and herbs.'
> This sister now cries out to us because of the harm we have inflicted on her by our irresponsible use and abuse of the goods with which God has endowed her. We have come to see ourselves as her lords and masters, entitled to plunder her at will.[3]

This personal, relational language used by the Pope to talk about the environment caught the imagination when the letter was published, months before the UN climate summit in 2015. It was addressed not only to Roman Catholics, Christians, people of faith and those of goodwill, but to every person on earth. In the care of our common home, we all need to be involved with the ecology and economy of the one planet where we live together, ecumenically.

The 'eco' of ecumenism, economy and ecology is interlinked. *Eco* in Greek means 'house'. *Meno* in Greek is 'to stay, dwell or abide'. Combined with *eco*, ecumenism is how we abide together in one house. *Nomos* in Greek means 'law', so economy means 'the laws of the house'. We have got used to thinking of ecology as the science of the relations between organisms to one another and their physical surroundings, but the Greek root of ecology is *logos*, meaning 'word'. For Christians, Logos is the creative Word of God at the opening of John's Gospel: 'In the beginning was the Word, and the Word was with God, and the Word was God' (1.1). For John, Jesus is the creative Word. 'In him was life, and the life was the light of all people' (1.4). John expresses our Advent hope that 'the light shines in the darkness, and the darkness did not overcome it' (1.5).

In *Laudato si'*, Pope Francis issued an urgent appeal for a new dialogue about the human roots of the environmental challenge that is shaping the future of our planet. He describes key indicators of the damage we are doing to our common home through the depletion of natural resources, and through the level of consumption in developed countries and the wealthier sectors of society, where the habit of wasting and discarding has reached unprecedented levels. The impact of these affects us all, because the pollution, climate change and loss of biodiversity is global.

The care of creation will not be just a technical fix, important though that is. When the carbon footprint of the richest 1 per cent is equivalent to that of the poorest 50 per cent, there are moral issues involved. How we live together in our common home ought to shape public policy and personal lifestyles. The faith communities have a strong commitment to environmental justice: we want to live more justly as well as more lightly on the earth.

The reflections of Pope Francis are both joyful and disturbing. He is issuing a stark warning about the spiritual nature of the problem and the seriousness of the crisis we face. Speaking in September 2020, the Pope addressed the two related themes of the pandemic and the environment. He said that to emerge from a pandemic, we need to look after and care for one another, especially the poor and most vulnerable. To get through the climate crisis, we must extend this care to our common home – to the earth and to every creature. The pope said that the best antidote to this misuse of our common home is contemplation: 'If someone has not learned to stop and admire something beautiful, we should not be surprised if he or she treats everything as an object to be used and abused without scruple.' In order to discover the true value of creation, 'We need to be silent, we need to listen, and we need to contemplate . . . Contemplating and caring: these are two attitudes that show the way to correct and rebalance our relationship as human beings with creation.'[4]

A prayer for our earth
All-powerful God, you are present in the whole universe
and in the smallest of your creatures.
You embrace with your tenderness all that exists.
Pour out upon us the power of your love,
that we may protect life and beauty.
Fill us with peace, that we may live
as brothers and sisters, harming no one.
O God of the poor,
help us to rescue the abandoned
and forgotten of this earth,
so precious in your eyes.
Bring healing to our lives,
that we may protect the world and not prey on it,
that we may sow beauty,
not pollution and destruction.
(Part of a prayer at the end of *Laudato si'*)

Friday

Letters for creation

There are something like 2.2 billion Christians in the world. The Church is local everywhere and is one of relatively few globally connected bodies. As the Church, we relate as friends and family 'in communion', sharing the life God has given us. We learn from one another, becoming better able to understand what is happening to the world in which we live.

With about 80 million members, the Anglican Communion is a relatively small part of the global Christian body, but it is a gift by which many schools, churches and every diocese have developed partnerships with people in other parts of the world. One of the things that brings home the reality of climate change is when people we know tell us what is happening in their communities. Before the pandemic, the ease of travel meant these partnerships were often experienced first-hand through visiting one another. For almost 50 years, my former Diocese of Salisbury has had a link with what is now the Sudan and South Sudan, countries not on many people's bucket list to visit. It is an extraordinarily strong bond in Christ. The stories of people we have got to know make a deep impact on us, perhaps particularly in a pandemic when we are physically apart, though remaining well connected.

In 2022, the care of God's creation was a main theme of the Lambeth Conference of all the bishops from the Anglican Communion, postponed a year because of the pandemic. In 2018, as part of the preparations, the Archbishop of Canterbury invited the Primate (the senior Archbishop in each of the Communion's 41 provinces) to write about what the care of God's creation means in their part of the world. These 'Letters for Creation' give insights into how climate change is being experienced differently around the world.[5]

From Polynesia in the Pacific Ocean, Bishop Winston Halapua wrote:

Island nations are being impacted by sea level rising due to Climate Change. Tuvalu, Kiribati and the Marshall Islands are threatened with non-existence as the sea level rises and land becomes uninhabitable. In Fiji, many villages are having to be relocated. In the Tongan island Pangaimotu, where as a boy I used to fish with my father, coconut palms stand stripped of fronds as the salt water encroaches and eats at root systems below the earth and cyclones ravage above.

The Archbishop of Cape Town, Thabo Makgoba, wrote:

In Southern Africa we are dependent on water for life – and climate change is changing rain patterns. On the eastern coast of southern Africa, Mozambique has been devastated by flooding. In contrast, in Namibia, Swaziland and South Africa the greatest impact has been that of crippling drought. Schools in parts of Swaziland had to be closed when they ran out of water for school toilets. In northern Namibia and southern Angola, people have been forced to slaughter their cattle, destroying their future economic stability.

Archbishop Paul Kwong from Hong Kong wrote that his city

faces enormous challenges to do with housing, clean water, environmental protection, ecological and bio-diversity, and climatic pollution. In these respects Hong Kong is particularly vexed by its situation: not only as part of the most populous nation on earth – China – in the most economically diverse continent – Asia – but also as a port on the shores of the busiest shipping lanes in the world . . . Truly caring for our city and our part of creation means being part of the way forward and part of its future. Our mission is to God's kingdom in the midst of this world: being God's companions means walking these same streets and living in these endlessly crowded communities, with and for one another.

Archbishop Zacharie Masimango Katanda, from Kindu in the Democratic Republic of the Congo, wrote:

A true ecological approach always becomes a social approach; it must integrate questions of justice in debates on the environment, so as to hear both the cry of the earth and the cry of the poor. The environment is God's gift to everyone, and in our use of it we have a responsibility towards the poor, towards future generations and towards humanity as a whole . . . Changes in lifestyle based on traditional moral virtues can ease the way to a sustainable and equitable world economy in which sacrifice will no longer be an unpopular concept. For many of us, a life less focused on material gain may remind us that we are more than what we have. Rejecting the false promises of excessive or conspicuous consumption can even allow more time for family, friends, and civic responsibilities. A renewed sense of sacrifice and restraint could make an essential contribution to addressing global climate change.

Advent is a time to face the truth about ourselves. It is also a time to review the way we live. Jesus summarized the Law as 'Love God and love your neighbour as yourself'. Our neighbour is not just family, or people from the same tribe, or the people we are physically close to, but everyone – the poor, the sick, the prisoner, the outcast, *everyone*. How do we live sustainably together in our common home? Being part of the worldwide Church helps us listen to our neighbours and see the impact of climate and environmental change in their lives. Church is a considerable resource in our learning to live locally and globally.

If your church has international links, ask your partners what the care of God's creation means to them. They will help us understand the writing on the wall . . .

The earth is the LORD's and all that is in it,
    the world, and those who live in it;
for he has founded it on the seas,
    and established it on the rivers.
Who shall ascend the hill of the LORD?
    And who shall stand in his holy place?
Those who have clean hands and pure hearts,
    who do not lift up their souls to what is false,
    and do not swear deceitfully.

They will receive blessing from the LORD,
 and vindication from the God of their salvation.
Such is the company of those who seek him,
 who seek the face of the God of Jacob.
(Ps. 24)

Saturday

Noah's ark

The drama of the preparation of Noah's ark in Genesis chapters 6–10 is captured in this painting by Margaret Gere. The energy and action are evident. Noah and his sons, their wives and children are at full stretch. The downpour has not yet come but already the impact of the impending flood is cross-generational. Most will be left behind as Noah gathers his household and pairs of every kind of creature into the ark to save them from the flood, which is God's judgement.

The company took stores to feed them for what would turn out to be almost a year. When the waters began to subside, Noah released a dove, which came back with an olive leaf as a sign that the flood was nearly over. God's new covenant with all creation was signalled by a rainbow, which has become a universal symbol that everyone belongs – we are God's diverse multicoloured rainbow people!

If the threat of being overwhelmed by a flood is universal, so is being ridiculed. It is easy to imagine onlookers scoffing as Noah built the ark. It has been said, 'All truth passes through three stages. First, it is ridiculed. Second, it is violently opposed. Third, it is accepted as being self-evident.' A flood doesn't seem real until it's too late. The same with climate change. There are still those who think we should not be organizing our lives and the economy around the threat of this. Of course, it is possible the science is wrong, or that we are over-reacting, but if our doctor diagnosed a sickness with 99 per cent certainty, most of us would take the medicine prescribed. If we continue as we are and the climate-change sceptics are wrong, it will be too late when we know for certain. If the climate scientists are wrong, the worst that will happen is that we will more renewable energy and a cleaner planet.

In my lifetime, the picture that has most changed the way we think about ourselves is *Earth Rise*, the photograph taken by the crew of the *Apollo 8* spacecraft on Christmas Eve 1968, when they became the first humans to witness the earth rising above the moon's barren surface. Fifty years after taking the photograph, William Anders observed, 'We set out to explore the moon and instead discovered the earth.' This blue planet is our beautiful, small, wondrous, fragile home, like an ark on which we dwell. Even in a vast expanding universe, there is no Planet B for us. This is it and we have a duty to care for the earth, for ourselves, for our successors, for life, for God.

At the turn of the millennium, the Royal Botanic Gardens at Kew developed a Noah's ark-like seed bank at Wakehurst in Sussex. With over a fifth of the planet's plant species at risk of extinction, they are gathering seeds from around the world in vaults that are bomb- and radiation-proof – an ever-growing store of more than 2.4 billion seeds.

God gave Noah directions, but it must have been difficult for him to decide which creatures to take into the ark and which to leave behind. In our day, we know about the importance of biodiversity and especially of pollinators, but

I would have thought twice about sharing space with wasps and mosquitos. There is a balance to be struck, and our choices make a difference for better and for worse. How do we decide what to protect, and is that choice always to be made on the basis of what is best for humans?

The story of Noah is foundational for the people of the Book: Jews, Christians and Muslims. It is a frightening narrative, though a very popular one, especially with children – not only are the animals attractive, but Noah's ark navigates danger safely and all ends well with God's rainbow covenant. The story is about how people, animals and plants survive and thrive together. Our human responsibility under God is to safeguard the integrity of creation and sustain and renew the life of the earth.

In this first week of Advent, we have been seeking to understand the meaning of the writing on the wall and wake up to the climate crisis that is upon us. The crisis has implications for us and for future generations, so a children's song is a good way to end the week.

From the tiny ant
From the tiny ant
To the elephant,
from the snake to the kangaroo;
From the great white shark
to the singing lark,
care for them it's up to you.
No one else will care for them
it's up, it's up,
it's up to you.

From the tabby cat
to the desert rat,
from the hamster to the chimpanzee;
from the common tern
to the crawling worm,
care for them it's up to me.
No one else will care for them
it's up, it's up,
it's up to me.

From the mongrel dog
to the snorting hog,
from the badger to the platypus;
from the small minnow
to the white rhino,
care for them it's up to us.
No one else will care for them
it's up, it's up,
it's up to us.
(Each line is repeated as a response to the lead singer)[6]

Jesus said, 'Let the little children come to me, and do not stop them; for it is to such as these that the kingdom of heaven belongs' (Matt. 19.14).

Questions for Week 1

- What struck you from the material this week?
- The facts about climate change and the environment are clear. Why do you think it is so difficult for us to address them?
- What would you say to our successors about the way we are handling climate change and environmental crises? What would you like to be able to say?
- What do you think will help wake us up to the scale of climate change and environmental crises?

WEEK 2

Midnight's solemn hour is tolling,
And seraph-notes are onward rolling;
They call on us our part to take.

Advent 2

Finding our place

When I was asked about becoming Bishop of Salisbury, I went to look at a painting of the cathedral by John Constable then in the National Gallery, just across the road from St Martin-in-the-Fields where I was the vicar. The painting helped me to imagine the transition from being a vicar to becoming a bishop, from living in central London to abiding in the real fields of Wiltshire and Dorset in the Diocese of Salisbury. It helped me to find my place and accept the part to which I was called.

John and Maria Constable were married in 1816 in St Martin's. They stayed in Salisbury and at Osmington near Weymouth with their friends Archdeacon John Fisher and his wife Mary, the archdeacon having conducted their wedding. Visits to these friends resulted in many sketches and paintings. The archdeacon's uncle, also John Fisher, was Bishop of Salisbury from 1807 to 1825, and Constable's patron. This painting of Salisbury Cathedral was a wedding present from Bishop John and his wife to their daughter.

In the painting, the bishop and his wife are walking in the garden of what was then the Bishop's Palace and is now the grounds of the cathedral school. Having been there by then for 16 years, they must have hoped the painting would be a reminder of the home their daughter had grown up in and was now leaving. She is pictured on the path ahead, separate from her parents. The bishop had expressed the opinion that, for a wedding present, there should be no dark clouds in the sky. Constable's response was that clouds were needed for the cathedral to be seen at its best, but he wanted to please the bishop, so a second version was painted with white clouds and blue sky. The clouds give some sense of reality in this privileged setting. No marriage is a cloudless sky but is 'for better for worse, for richer for poorer, in sickness and in health'. Poignantly, Constable's wife Maria was developing tuberculosis, from which she would die in 1828, aged only 41.

One way and another, it was a tricky commission and a relief to Constable when he was able to write, 'My Cathedral looks very well. Indeed I got through that job uncommonly well considering how much I dreaded it . . . It was the most difficult subject in landscape I ever had on my easel.'[1]

The interplay between the cathedral and the garden is delightful, although the trees can't ever have been exactly as painted! They are shaped like Gothic arches, making space for this fine view of the tallest spire in England, pointing to God and earthing heaven. The bishop was known to be a vain man, and it has been suggested that pointing his stick at the cathedral implies he (as bishop) is master of all he surveys. However, it never felt like that to me, and I doubt it did to John Fisher. Standing beside the cathedral always gave me a sense of how much bigger it was than any of us, and that is what is depicted by the relative size of the bishop and his family.

Salisbury Cathedral is one of the most glorious buildings in the world. Nowadays, it is interpreted by three great contemporary works of art. Christianity begins with baptism, so the cathedral is entered by passing William Pye's large font, with its still, reflective surface and water flowing from four spouts. Those gathering for worship look towards the east window by Gabriel Loire, dedicated to prisoners of conscience, which speaks of the Isaiah agenda with which Jesus announced his ministry in the Nazareth synagogue:

'The Spirit of the Lord is upon me, because he has anointed me to bring good news to the poor. He has sent me to proclaim release to the captives and recovery of sight to the blind, to let the oppressed go free, to proclaim the year of the Lord's favour.'
(Luke 4.18–19)

Outside the cathedral is Elisabeth Frink's statue *Walking Madonna*. The mother of Christ is walking towards the city, away from the cathedral dedicated in her name, and there is energy and determination in her stride. Like any church, Salisbury Cathedral is a place in which we find ourselves in relation to God, to one another and to all creation. Our calling, like Mary's, is to go out and take our part in the work God calls us to for the kingdom.

The care of creation is an important and integral part of our Christian witness in the world. One of the best ways for churches to develop a care for creation is through entering the Eco Church awards of the Christian environmental charity A Rocha. Churches, cathedrals and dioceses – as well as synagogues and mosques – can work progressively for bronze, silver and gold awards, and so start a journey that is motivated by a desire to do the right thing and helped by friendly competition. Hilfield Friary in Dorset, in the Diocese of Salisbury, was the first to receive a gold award. Salisbury was the first diocese to receive a bronze. In 2020, the cathedral installed 93 solar panels on the cloister roof, generating clean energy and reducing the building's carbon footprint. Gloucester Cathedral had earlier installed solar panels, but Salisbury was the first cathedral to receive a gold award. Many churches are now engaged in the Eco Church process, and several are already carbon neutral.

Eco Church is not the only way for a church to further the care of God's creation, but if your church is not involved, perhaps ask why it isn't.

Isaiah has a prophetic vision:

A shoot shall come out from the stock of Jesse,
and a branch shall grow out of his roots.
The spirit of the Lord shall rest on him,
the spirit of wisdom and understanding,
the spirit of counsel and might,
the spirit of knowledge and the fear of the Lord.
His delight shall be in the fear of the Lord.
He shall not judge by what his eyes see,
or decide by what his ears hear;
but with righteousness he shall judge the poor,
and decide with equity for the meek of the earth;
he shall strike the earth with the rod of his mouth,
and with the breath of his lips he shall kill the wicked.
Righteousness shall be the belt around his waist,
and faithfulness the belt around his loins.
The wolf shall live with the lamb,
the leopard shall lie down with the kid,
the calf and the lion and the fatling together,
and a little child shall lead them.
The cow and the bear shall graze,

their young shall lie down together;
    and the lion shall eat straw like the ox.
The nursing child shall play over the hole of the asp,
    and the weaned child shall put its hand on the adder's den.
They will not hurt or destroy
    on all my holy mountain;
for the earth will be full of the knowledge of the LORD
    as the waters cover the sea.
On that day the root of Jesse shall stand as a signal to the peoples; the
nations shall inquire of him, and his dwelling shall be glorious.
(Is. 11.1–10)

Monday

Forgiveness and thanksgiving

Given its name, the Eden Project in Cornwall is an oddly secular environmental project and visitor attraction. It was created in an old China clay pit, with the aim of building relationships between people and the natural world, and to demonstrate the power of working together for the benefit of all living things. Its co-founder, Sir Tim Smit, said:

> In the beginning the idea was very simple. Let's take a place of utter dereliction and create life in it and in that place also demonstrate how clever Homo sapiens is technologically in terms of being able to answer a whole series of problems to create life wherever you are . . . We are morphing now into a position where we realise that the environment needs now to be positioned not as being political, either left wing or right wing, but existentially we all need to embrace the notion of survival being based on having clean air, clean water, fertile soils and a degree of much greater equity around sharing those resources. Eden is now firmly based in that space wanting to demonstrate how we can be a circular ecology in a circular economy.[2]

In this, they are helping to chart the way for the rest of us. The Eden Project's ten top tips for living sustainably include things such as: don't waste; learn about your life; imagine different things; forgive yourself (and others); be hopeful; give gifts and give thanks. Some of these could have come from a letter in the New Testament! But while its name links the Eden Project strongly with the Bible, it nurtures what is perceived to be good without the need for religious roots.

In the late twentieth century, the German Roman Catholic theologian Hans Küng wrote about 'global ethics' and what is universally thought to be good. In a diverse world, we have to find language, thought and action common to us all that is capable of sustaining life. Thanksgiving by implication is sacred because thanks is being given to someone, whereas a secular thankfulness can be a person's attitude. Either way, there is something universal about people being thankful.

Each faith has its own framework for what it is to be good. *Laudato si'*, mentioned earlier, quotes Patriarch Bartholomew, the 'Green Patriarch' of Constantinople, on the need for each of us individually to repent of the ways we have harmed the planet and acknowledge our sins against creation. Forgiveness helps us turn around and find hope that leads to renewed life with thanksgiving. For Christians, this is nurtured and nourished by worship, the Scriptures, sacraments and fellowship of the Church. Penitence, forgiveness and thanksgiving are at the heart of the Christian way.

The first parish in which I served as the vicar was on the Isle of Dogs, the loop in the River Thames familiar from the title sequence of *EastEnders* on TV. In Advent and Lent, we used the Ten Commandments to introduce the Confession. On the first occasion, the driver for the Kray brothers (notorious gangsters in the 1950s and 60s), who had served ten years in prison for a murder he claimed not to have committed, said as he left church, 'I haven't heard those commandments since I was a child. I have broken nine and I am not going to tell you which is the tenth.'

When I moved to St Martin-in-the-Fields, I continued introducing the Confession in this way during Advent and Lent, and one of the congregation asked why I associated the Commandments with penitence. She said that keeping the Commandments is a joyful way of living, involving not penitence but thanksgiving. In fact, both responses are valid. The Commandments offer a way of living and they also show us where we have fallen short. Confession leads to absolution and to a profound thankfulness for the forgiveness of sins, which helps shape our relationships. Then we try again to do better, to live by the Commandments and live up to the glory of God.

The central act of worship in church is variously described in words that signal different emphases: Holy Communion, the Eucharist or the Mass. Holy Communion speaks of our 'at oneness', the Mass of our being dismissed at the end of the service and sent out to join in the work of God in the world.

The Eucharist means thanksgiving, praising God for the gifts of creation and redemption. Central to this is the memory that

in the same night that he was betrayed
[Jesus] took bread and gave you thanks;
he broke it and gave it to his disciples, saying:
Take, eat; this is my body which is given for you;
do this in remembrance of me.[3]

Thanksgiving when being betrayed and broken? This is not a denial of harsh realities but an acknowledgement and acceptance of them. We take and eat the gift of the body of Christ's transformative power, and live as people who see things differently and can still give thanks for everything. For whatever reason, receiving with thanksgiving bestows on us great freedom. In the words of the Eucharistic Prayer, 'It is our duty and our joy, at all times . . . to give [God] thanks and praise.'[4] And thus we find the confidence to take our part in seeking to heal the earth.

The seventeenth-century Anglican priest and poet Thomas Traherne wrote:

Your enjoyment of the world is never right, till every morning you awake in Heaven; see yourself in your Father's Palace; and look upon the skies, the earth, and the air as Celestial Joys: having such a reverend esteem of all, as if you were among the Angels.[5]

St Paul links these two themes of forgiveness and thanksgiving in his instruction to Christians:

As God's chosen ones, holy and beloved, clothe yourselves with compassion, kindness, humility, meekness, and patience. Bear with one another and, if anyone has a complaint against another, forgive each other; just as the Lord has forgiven you, so you also must forgive. Above all, clothe yourselves with love, which binds everything together in perfect harmony. And let the peace of Christ rule in your hearts, to which indeed you were called in the one body. And be thankful. Let the word of Christ dwell in you richly; teach and admonish one another in all wisdom; and with gratitude in your hearts sing psalms, hymns, and spiritual songs to God. And whatever you do, in word or deed, do everything in the name of the Lord Jesus, giving thanks to God the Father through him.

(Col. 3:12–17)

Tuesday

St Nicholas

The 6 December is St Nicholas Day. A number of other marvellous saints are remembered in Advent, but none makes as big an impact at this time of year as St Nick, from whom Santa Claus is derived. As his name is also my name, I want to remember him today with this icon from St Catherine's Monastery at the foot of Mount Sinai in Egypt.

In the fourth century, Nicholas was Bishop of Myra in modern Turkey. In Greek his name means 'victory of the people', and there are stories about Nicholas the wonder-worker, performing miracles or sometimes just small acts of kindness. Each was a victory for the people: he calmed a storm, saving the lives of sailors; he brought back to life three boys, killed during a famine by a butcher and pickled in brine to be sold; he threw three bags of gold coins through a window as a dowry for three girls about to be sold by their poor father.

As a child, I sang in Benjamin Britten's *Saint Nicolas* cantata, music celebrating his life through stories like the above, some of which are depicted on the icon. I was never the child saint in the opening section, but several times I sang as one of the three pickled boys brought back to life, repeatedly singing 'Alleluia!'. When I became a bishop, I included three bags of gold on my episcopal seal to remind me and those I served of the generosity of St Nicholas, and the life-saving impact of his anonymous gifts to save the three girls. Saints show us what it means for us to be good. As people close to God, they make life so much better for everyone by their example. I am not perfect, but at my best I want to be a saint. That desire gives my life direction – ambition as well as hope.

St Nicholas became one of the most popular saints in Europe. In England, he is the patron saint of over 500 parish churches. In the Netherlands, on the eve of St Nicholas Day, *Sinterklaas* passes through locked doors or comes down chimneys to leave gifts in shoes and stockings for the children. There are special markets selling toys and biscuits shaped like St Nicholas, and impersonators dressed in red bishop's costumes. It's easy to see how this tradition got amalgamated in the nineteenth century with the medieval personification of Christmas, who became the gift-giving Santa Claus.

My favourite annual service as Bishop of Salisbury was the cathedral evensong on the Sunday nearest St Nicholas Day. In keeping with a medieval tradition, my place as bishop was taken by a child, one of the choristers. Each year I placed a mitre on the child's head and a ring on his or her finger. The child sat on the bishop's throne – which in Salisbury is big – while I disrobed and sat on a chair. The choir sang the Magnificat:

> He hath showed strength with his arm: he hath scattered the proud, in
>   the imagination of their hearts.
> He hath put down the mighty from their seat: and hath exalted the
>   humble and meek.
> He hath filled the hungry with good things: and the rich he hath sent
>   empty away.[6]

The child bishop preached the sermon. The ten I heard in my time were all brilliant. It was a humbling experience – not in a demeaning kind of way but in one that was profoundly humanizing. I was reminded of who I am as a person and, like any parent, I was delighted to be taught by a child.

The ways in which we speak about climate change and environmental degradation often include asking what we will we say to our grandchildren if we fail because we did not do enough. It's a good question. We can all see that we are giving succeeding generations a very difficult set of problems. But I am now of an age when my children and their children are talking quite a lot about climate change and the environment. Every school is on the case. A primary school in Dorset organized a 'climate summit' and brought neighbouring schools together to tell me what they had found out and ask me what I was doing about it. On these issues, we need to listen to our children and feel what the care of God's creation means to them.

It is often said that Christmas is for the children. Spend some time looking at the icon and thinking about the generosity of St Nicholas. What would it mean for us to be generous to our children and theirs, the next generations?

What have children to say to us about the way we have cared for God's creation? When you are next with children, ask them what they think about climate change and the environment. As we prepare for Christmas, what are the gifts you most want for the young people you love?

Advent Calendar
He will come like last leaf's fall.
One night when the November wind
has flayed the trees to the bone, and earth
wakes choking on the mould,
the soft shroud's folding.

He will come like frost.
One morning when the shrinking earth
opens on mist, to find itself
arrested in the net
of alien, sword-set beauty.

He will come like dark.
One evening when the bursting red
December sun draws up the sheet
and penny-masks its eye to yield
the star-snowed fields of sky.

He will come, will come,
will come like crying in the night,
like blood, like breaking,
as the earth writhes to toss him free.
He will come like child.
(Rowan Williams, b. 1950)[7]

Wednesday

Twelve Steps

I am Nicholas and I am addicted to fossil fuels. I am not the only person for whom this is true. The geopolitical difficulties we face in the supply of oil and gas, particularly since the war in Ukraine and European dependency on Russian gas, and the highly charged debates about the role of fossil fuels in our making the transition to carbon neutrality by 2050 (think 'leave it in the ground' because we know it is damaging and need renewables when the way we live continues to depend on the use of oil and gas) make it clear that this is not just my problem.

I sometimes wonder if environmental spirituality is a bit like the spirituality of Alcoholics Anonymous (AA) and the other Twelve Steps groups that have developed from it to combat addictions. This spirituality teaches that we won't be sufficiently determined to get our lives back on track unless we recognize our circumstances are so serious that we have reached rock bottom and things simply can't get any worse. Unless we acknowledge the mess we are in, and our need for a power greater than our own, along with the support and solidarity of others, we will not be able to work our way to recovery.

AA say their programme operates when recovering alcoholics pass on the story of their own problem drinking, describe the sobriety they have found in AA, and invite newcomers to join the informal fellowship. Its evangelical purpose helps the evangelist perhaps more than the evangelized. The Twelve Steps describe the experience of the earliest members:

1　We admitted we were powerless over alcohol – that our lives had become unmanageable.
2　Came to believe that a Power greater than ourselves could restore us to sanity.

3 Made a decision to turn our will and our lives over to the care of God as we understood Him.

4 Made a searching and fearless moral inventory of ourselves.

5 Admitted to God, to ourselves, and to another human being the exact nature of our wrongs.

6 Were entirely ready to have God remove all these defects of character.

7 Humbly asked Him to remove our shortcomings.

8 Made a list of all persons we had harmed, and became willing to make amends to them all.

9 Made direct amends to such people wherever possible, except when to do so would injure them or others.

10 Continued to take personal inventory and when we were wrong promptly admitted it.

11 Sought through prayer and meditation to improve our conscious contact with God as we understood Him, praying only for knowledge of His will for us and the power to carry that out.

12 Having had a spiritual awakening as the result of these Steps, we tried to carry this message to alcoholics and to practice these principles in all our affairs.[8]

Newcomers to AA are not asked to accept or follow these Twelve Steps in their entirety if they feel unwilling or unable to do so. They will usually be asked to keep an open mind, to attend meetings at which recovered alcoholics describe their personal experiences in achieving sobriety, and to read AA literature describing and interpreting the AA programme.

The Twelve Steps may be a useful way for some of us to think about how we could live in relation to our use of carbon, particularly those who experience climate-change anxiety to the extent that they feel life has become unmanageable. For everyone, the Steps are a practical framework for addressing personal change. Our society depends on fossil fuels, and for the time being at least it is almost impossible for us to live without them – as queues at the petrol station in any fuel crisis demonstrate. Even something as simple as attempting a plastic-free Lent defeated me. The exercise became more of an educational one about how much plastic we use and the often not-so-good alternatives that are available.

Try noticing today how much fossil fuel you use, directly and indirectly, and what sort of alternatives are available. We have a very long way to go to change our lifestyles. The move away from carbon is definitely going to involve sacrifice.

The prayer of Alcoholics Anonymous is helpful for all of us who are ready to stop being complacent and take action. It is based on a prayer of the American Protestant theologian, Reinhold Niebuhr:

God, grant us grace to accept the things we cannot change,
Courage to change the things we can change,
And wisdom to know the difference.

The original version of the prayer from which this is just the beginning continues:

Living one day at a time,
Enjoying one moment at a time,
Accepting hardship as the pathway to peace;
Taking, as He did, this sinful world as it is,
Not as I would have it;
Trusting that He will make all things right
If I surrender to His will;
That I may be reasonably happy in this life,
And supremely happy with Him for ever
In the next. Amen.
(Reinhold Niebuhr (1892–1971)

In Advent, Niebuhr's prayer reminds us of our condition, suspended as we are between the poles of wretchedness and glory. He recognizes that salvation is not in our own hands but that we are called to live in response to the fact of our salvation and not in our strength alone.

Thursday

Travelling together

Welcoming delegates to COP26, the UN Climate Change conference in Glasgow in November 2021, Prime Minister Boris Johnson said, 'It's one minute to midnight . . . and we need to act now. If we don't get serious about climate change today, it will be too late for our children to do so tomorrow.'

In Glasgow, a greater global urgency about climate change was generated, but what the prime minister said is pretty much what many political leaders have been expressing for years. The conference was a huge effort and the politicians are entitled to feel positive about its achievements. As mentioned earlier, it is estimated that projected global warming will reduce from about 3.7 degrees after Paris 2015 to possibly 2.7 degrees after Glasgow, but that is a long way short of 2 degrees, let alone 1.5. It was no surprise when Greta Thunberg described COP26 as 'Blah blah blah'. She and the climate activists were also right to regard the summit as a failure. We aren't grasping the scale or the urgency of the problems facing us.

We have just 27 years to meet the climate-change goals of the 2015 Paris Agreement. The size of the environmental challenge can feel overwhelming, simply too big to face – like judgement without the possibility that repentance and turning again will make a difference. When there is no hope, we are paralysed, because it becomes impossible to take our part and act meaningfully. It is not surprising that some people express what is called 'climate anxiety'. A mixture of futility and fear causes us to bury our heads in the sand. We despair.

Finding a way out of this requires a realistic framework, a collective plan and a great deal of effort. We must start individually, because doing the right thing makes a difference to who we are and the way we live. It's a matter of being true to ourselves. Each of us has a part to play and our individual actions become powerful when we use them collectively with others making similar choices. However, the big changes come at pace through public policy and good law. For example, the introduction of a small charge on single-use plastic bags in the UK reduced the number used from 7.69 billion in 2014 to 550 million in 2019, a drop of over 85 per cent.

Legislation needs consent and there has to be widespread trust that it is in our best interests. Business needs to be sure the legislative framework can be relied on and isn't going to change repeatedly. For example, the introduction of electric vehicles depends on large-scale investment. That would not be made without the assurance that by 2030 no new petrol or diesel cars or vans will be sold in the UK, and that the rest of the world is making the same transition at a similar if not identical pace. The development of an infrastructure to provide easily accessible charging is also needed. How this happens is likely to change as the technology develops. When video recorders were first available, there were two main but incompatible systems. Now no one uses video recorders and we cast programmes to TV from our smart phones.

Time is short. We're convinced about the need for change without being sure exactly what to do. Greta Thunberg said that what is required is 'cathedral thinking'. I think she meant that we need a big vision and must begin without knowing exactly how things will turn out. The tasks are urgent. We may not tackle them in exactly the right way, but we must act now and make our mistakes in the right direction.

Each person has a part to play, but we need our best scientists, business leaders, politicians, faith leaders and community activists – our greatest souls – to work with common purpose, because we belong together. The relationships between us will often be strained as we move towards an agreed but still not uncontested goal. Thinking of the traditional Advent themes of death, judgement, heaven and hell in relation to climate change and the environment may cause anxiety, but that same anxiety can inspire innovation and hope.

A mature spirituality helps us to hold our anxiety without the need for fight or flight. It leads to the growth of character, behaviour and experience that enables us to act, individually and together, in responding to climate change. Remember the notion of living simply so that others may simply live? It is worth holding on to this, as although the urgency of innovation is exciting, change will take longer than we would like and some of what we hope for won't work.

There is a certain resonance with the biblical story of the exodus. Less than three months after fleeing from Egypt, the Israelites were grumbling about Moses and Aaron leading the people into the wilderness to starve to death. They remembered having enough food in Egypt. At least if they had died there, they would not have been hungry. It was better to be slaves in Egypt, they said, than lost in the desert of Sinai. God heard their complaints and provided manna from heaven and quail's eggs.

It took 40 years for Israel to journey from slavery in Egypt to the freedom of the promised land – in other words, more than a generation to forget the experience of slavery, stop looking back and be ready for all that was new. We do not have that long.

In relation to our use of fossil fuels we know it's time to move on, and we know we need to do this together. I love this prayer based on words of Dag Hammarskjöld (1905–61), United Nations Secretary-General.

For all that has been – thanks.
To all that will be – yes.[9]

Friday

Fear or love?

What motivates us more: fear or love?

The life, death and resurrection of Jesus teach us to love. He summarized the Law as loving God and loving your neighbour as yourself. Such love is not sentimental. In what Jesus said and did, he made it clear that our neighbour includes the stranger and the outcast, even our enemy. We are neighbours to one another and that means to everyone, no exceptions. Love is self-giving and sacrificial: 'No one has greater love than this, to lay down one's life for one's friends' (John 15.13).

St Paul wrote that for the time being we know things partially, but when we see face to face and know as we are fully known, the three things that abide are faith, hope and love – and the greatest is love (1 Cor. 13.12–13). According to St John, 'perfect love casts out fear' (1 John 4.18).

It seems obvious to extend Jesus' summary of the Law to include the love of creation: love God, love your neighbour as yourself, and don't forget to love the world you've been given to care for. This is language that motivates faith communities, not only Christians. In preparation for the 2015 UN Climate Change summit, churches and development agencies said we cared about the climate 'For the Love of . . .' Mothers, children, farmers, surfers, Morris dancers said they cared about the climate 'For the Love of . . .' There is no more powerful motivation. Love is universal, and for the love of our children and grandchildren, for the love of creation, for the love of God, people getting serious about climate change find energy and hope.

Since the summit, we have had a pandemic and it was extraordinary how quickly and how radically we changed our lifestyles as we (mostly) followed the advice given and kept the regulations. With so little traffic, and planes largely on the ground, the air cleared. Did we do it 'For the Love of . . .'? In some ways we did. We were concerned to protect ourselves and one another and to save the NHS from being overwhelmed. We didn't want to catch or pass on a dangerous, little understood virus that medics were only learning to treat and for which there was no vaccine. But it was not only love that changed our behaviour. There was an element of fear too.

Now we are living with the virus and keen to rebuild the economy, the temptation is to try to go back to things as they were. The airline industry wants us to fly as much as we did. The motor industry wants us to drive again and buy more cars. But if we do so, we will miss the big opportunity to 'build back better'. Transport is becoming more efficient, but it will be decades before aircraft are carbon neutral. The increase in video conferencing during the pandemic has meant we have accepted there is less need for business travel when we can meet online.

Most people enjoy international holidays, but it would help if we were more fearful about the damage we are doing to the environment by flying. Aviation makes up 7 per cent of the UK's greenhouse gas emissions, yet few people are aware that aviation kerosene is not taxed due to international agreement. The missing tax is made up for to some extent by the level of Air Passenger Duty, but in 2021 the UK's chancellor cut this by 50 per cent on domestic flights to encourage us to fly. It is crazy that it is cheaper to fly from Manchester to London than to go by train. It would be simple to have Air Passenger Duty increase with the number of flights we take each year. Some travellers have begun adding the cost of carbon off-setting to the cost of a journey by whatever means, but what is needed is realistic carbon pricing.

When we know there is a climate emergency, doing things 'For the Love of . . .' means reducing our carbon emissions from travel as much as we did during the pandemic, and to continue to do this every year for the next ten years. Such action requires a spirituality that is self-disciplined, reverent and concerned with sustainability. A bit of fear is healthy for us – the sort of fear that is not the opposite of love, but rather a humility, a restraint through which we find our place as creatures in relation to our Creator. Such characteristics will make it more possible to be part of a sustainable creation, rather than one that exhausts, depletes and pollutes through continuous consumption.

'The fear of the LORD is the beginning of wisdom.'
(Prov. 9.10)

Saturday

The beauty of holiness

Pope Francis suggested that we should stop to admire something beautiful and that contemplation will prevent us from treating everything as something to be used. Losing – or finding – ourselves in the beauty of holiness, and recognizing the holiness of beauty, will encourage in us the kind of reverence for life we need if we are to take our part in the global response to the climate emergency.

The tapestry in this picture is by Gerhard Richter, one of our greatest contemporary artists. He describes himself as an atheist with leanings towards Catholicism, which is a bit like the novelist Julian Barnes saying that he doesn't believe in God but does miss him. In church circles, Richter is best known for his huge stained-glass window in Cologne Cathedral (2007) – an abstract collage of 11,500 pixel-like squares in 72 colours, randomly arranged by computer. The then Archbishop of Cologne reportedly did not like it, which is a reminder that the Church may curate a space, but it does not entirely control the narrative to which people contribute. Great art creates controversy. Richter gives us a way of seeing that invites a response.

Many of Richter's paintings are produced by spreading paint and mirroring the design created, as with paint and a paper fold. This tapestry has four quarters repeating an abstract pattern. Looking at a photograph of it is evocative, but not nearly as good as experiencing it first-hand. When the tapestry is viewed hanging in a chapel, most people see a cross with expanding energy at its centre. It is evident that the skill of the artist and of those who made the tapestry is awesome. Its spaciousness creates room for us to be still and to wonder. Doing so, I can avoid my own tendency to displacement activities. Contemplation allows us to hold together the complexities of life with fear and love.

Contemplation of that which God has made and given to us creates in us a reverence for life. The medieval mystic Mother Julian of Norwich saw God in an object the size of a hazelnut.

> I saw that [our Lord] is to us everything which is good and comforting for our help. He is our clothing, who wraps and enfolds us for love, embraces us and shelters us, surrounds us for his love, which is so tender that he may never desert us. And so in this sight I saw that he is everything which is good, as I understand.
>
> And in this he showed me a little thing, the quantity of a hazelnut, lying in the palm of my hand, it seemed, and it was as round as any ball. I looked thereupon with the eye of my understanding, and I thought, 'What may this be?' And it was answered generally thus: 'It is all that is made.' I wondered how it could last, for I thought it might suddenly fall to nothing for little cause. And I was answered in my understanding: 'It lasts and ever shall, for God loves it; and so everything has its beginning by the love of God.' In this little thing I saw three properties; the first is that God made it; the second is that God loves it; and the third is that God keeps it.[10]

Find something today that makes you pause and really look at its beauty.

Questions for Week 2

- What struck you from the material this week?
- What part do feelings of fear or love (or other emotions) play in your response to climate change and environmental crises?
- What is the sin (or sins) we need to repent of in relation to climate change?
- What progress are you making in finding your place and taking your part in the care of God's creation?

WEEK 3

Come forth, ye virgins wise:
The Bridegroom comes, arise!
Alleluia!

Advent 3

Being human

Every religion contains an account of what it is to be human.

Gossaert's painting of Adam and Eve captures the moment of their loss of innocence. Eve is hiding the apple, the serpent is coiled around the branch above her head and the garden of Eden is behind the couple. Having made a choice, they look upset but hold together under the two special trees in Eden – the tree of the knowledge of good and evil, and the tree of life. At the end of the day, when the Lord God comes looking for them in the garden, they hide as little children do. But there is no hiding place. Instead, they are consigned to the land where we now stand: a stony ground east of Eden, with a memory of paradise and a hope of heaven.

The interesting fact that there are two creation stories at the beginning of the book of Genesis makes clear that these are not to be regarded as science or history but as accounts of what it is to be human. For Jews and Christians these creation stories are seminal.

Genesis 1 tells the story of creation in six days: 'In the beginning . . . God created the heavens and the earth' (Gen. 1.1). On days two to five, what God made was good. On the sixth day God created humankind in God's image, male and female. God blessed them and gave them dominion over the fish of the sea, the birds of the air and every living thing that moves upon the earth, every green plant for food. 'God saw everything that he had made, and indeed, it was very good' (Gen. 1.31). We are made for goodness *and* we are given dominion.

Being given dominion over all creation has shaped the way human beings have understood themselves. It has encouraged us as a species to behave selfishly, as though creation is for us to use and consume. But within the Hebrew Scriptures, there are many texts that delight in the creation in and of itself, under the ultimate dominion of God, not simply because it serves human need. The best conservation and stewardship cares for the whole system for the good of all, particularly now we know that anthropocentrism is self-destructive. For Christians, dominion has to be understood in the light of the dominion of Christ, the servant Lord. It is not all about us. We live in relationship with other human beings and with the whole of creation. This is an ancient and embedded truth, not a novel contemporary insight. In our time, it matters more than ever.

The story of the creation in six days is followed by another story, about the creation of Adam and Eve, in Genesis 2 and 3. In Hebrew, Adam means 'man', or 'earth creature', linked to *Adamah*, earth. The name Eve is linked with the Hebrew word for life. So God forms the earth creatures out of the earth and animates them with the breath and spirit of life. These earth creatures are put into the garden of Eden to 'till it and keep it', which could be translated as to 'serve and conserve' the garden.

We creatures are tempted to want to be like God. Yet we find it difficult to take responsibility for our actions. When found out, the temptation is to hide and pass the blame, just as Adam blames Eve for giving him the apple, and she blames the serpent for tricking her. No scientific account of human nature could convey so well their feelings of guilt and shame. Adam and Eve are everyman and everywoman. Banished to a place east of Eden, they are consigned to a life of toil. The earth now gives them thorns and thistles, and producing more human beings involves the pains of childbirth. That is the human condition.

Our health and well-being depend on an ecology that supports the diversity of life. Few challenges have tested us as much as climate change and the environmental degradation of our day. We have eaten the fruit of the tree and must take responsibility for what we have done, being honest and truthful as we creatively work towards a new way of life. We cannot undertake this in our strength alone. St Paul describes Jesus Christ as the new Adam, the one uniquely full of God's Spirit, while in John's Gospel, Jesus brings life, the Greek *zoe* picking up the life of the Hebrew *Evach*, or Eve. Jesus is the creative Word who was with God before creation and abides with us. Not only does Jesus teach us to love God and love our neighbour; his death and resurrection make this transforming possibility a reality, as he demonstrates that the one who is greatest is the one who serves. Jesus redefines what it means to have dominion and restores our lost innocence so we may live as people who care lovingly for God's creation, like the Lord and Master who came to serve.

In the Advent imagery of the hymn 'Sleepers, Wake', 'The Bridegroom comes, arise!'

> The wilderness and the dry land shall be glad,
>   the desert shall rejoice and blossom;
> like the crocus it shall blossom abundantly,
>   and rejoice with joy and singing.
> The glory of Lebanon shall be given to it,
>   the majesty of Carmel and Sharon.
> They shall see the glory of the LORD,
>   the majesty of our God.
> (Is. 35.1–2)

Monday

Making the most of our talents

Johann Sebastian Bach was one of the world's greatest musicians. Yet when he was appointed to be in charge of music at the Church of St Thomas in Leipzig nearly 300 years ago, he was at least the third choice. Telemann and Graupner had turned the job down when their current employers significantly increased their salaries to retain them. So when Bach took the post in April 1723, he may have felt he had something to prove. His output is astonishing. In five years he wrote 150 cantatas, as well as *Magnificat* (1723), the *St John Passion* (1724) and the *St Matthew Passion* (1727). The musical resources of the church were limited: 16 first-choir singers and up to 18 instrumentalists. Cantatas were performed on Sundays at 7.30 a.m. The *Oxford Companion to Music* comments, 'It is not unlikely that some of the performances were poor.'[1] In 1730, increasingly disenchanted with the conditions at St Thomas's, Bach submitted a memorandum to the church authorities setting out his minimum requirements for well-regulated church music. Their response was to threaten to reduce his salary.

The 'Sleepers, Wake' cantata (BMV 140) was first performed on 25 November 1731, the Sunday before Advent. Hymnody and the reading of the Bible are central to Lutheran worship, as they were to the development of German identity and language. The text of the cantata is based on Philipp Nicolai's hymn 'Wachet auf' and was a response to the day's Gospel reading. It completed Bach's second cycle of cantatas at St Thomas's and had an urgency suitable for the end of the church's year (before the cycle began again the following Advent Sunday).

> Then the kingdom of heaven will be like this. Ten bridesmaids took their lamps and went to meet the bridegroom. Five of them were foolish, and five were wise. When the foolish took their lamps, they

took no oil with them; but the wise took flasks of oil with their lamps. As the bridegroom was delayed, all of them became drowsy and slept. But at midnight there was a shout, 'Look! Here is the bridegroom! Come out to meet him.' Then all those bridesmaids got up and trimmed their lamps. The foolish said to the wise, 'Give us some of your oil, for our lamps are going out.' But the wise replied, 'No! there will not be enough for you and for us; you had better go to the dealers and buy some for yourselves.' And while they went to buy it, the bridegroom came, and those who were ready went with him into the wedding banquet; and the door was shut. Later the other bridesmaids came also, saying, 'Lord, lord, open to us.' But he replied, 'Truly I tell you, I do not know you.' Keep awake therefore, for you know neither the day nor the hour.
(Mt. 25.1–13)

Much of the teaching of Jesus is in the form of stories that we cannot reduce to a series of propositions because they are much more about developing character and attitude. No one story is sufficient, but cumulatively we receive the gospel, the good news, of Jesus Christ. The account of the wise and foolish virgins is one of a series of stories Matthew groups together that are about the end of this age, judgement and the coming of the Son of Man. There is a fear of our being caught out and an urgency to our being prepared for the Lord's coming. In some ways, I wish the women had shared their lights and everyone had worked collectively to welcome the bridegroom, but that's not what is related. Rather, each had to be ready – even at midnight!

The story that follows in Matthew's Gospel is the parable of the talents. A man was going on a journey so he summoned his slaves and gave them his property to look after while he was away. To one he gave five talents, to another two, to another one, each according to his ability. The first traded with them and made five talents more and the second did similarly and doubled what he had, but the third was afraid and buried his one talent until the master returned. When the man came back, he praised the first two and said that because they had been trustworthy, he would give them more. The third returned what he had received but was told he was lazy and wicked for doing nothing with it, not even banking it so the master would get the interest. His talent was taken from him and given to those who had more than enough but knew how to use it. The already fearful slave was told he was worthless and cast into outer darkness. It is a hell of a story.

Life is tough in this mythical land east of Eden, where we live with a loss of innocence and have to work hard for our worthwhile achievements. It is a cliché, but it is true, that how we navigate the toughest things that happen to us makes us the people we become. This may be said of individuals and of groups. We are shaped by the challenges we surmount, not because we are all brilliant and get everything right, but because we know ourselves, are determined, develop our knowledge and abilities and act creatively. When we make the most of the gifts God has given us, we find we can do more than we ever imagined possible.

The third story in Matthew 25 is the parable of the sheep and the goats. Again, it is a parable about judgement and makes a division between those who saw Jesus in the hungry, thirsty, naked, stranger, sick and prisoner, and cared for them, and those who saw and did nothing: 'Truly I tell you, just as you did it to one of the least of these who are members of my family, you did it to me' (Mt. 25.40).

Matthew's Gospel speaks of knowing neither the day nor the hour, and these three stories call us to live with urgency and creativity rather than just coast along. That is very much the response we need to climate change and the environment. We can make the most of what we have for ourselves and the good of others. In doing so, we will know the joy in finding that God is with us – and we will become more fully human.

'Sleepers, Wake', verse 2
Zion hears the voice that singeth,
With sudden joy her glad heart springeth,
At once she wakes, she stands arrayed:
Her Light is come, her star ascending,
Lo, girt with truth, with mercy blending,
Her Bridegroom there, so long delayed.
All hail! God's glorious Son,
All hail! our joy and crown,
Alleluia! The joyful call, we answer all,
And follow to the bridal hall.
(P. Nicolai, 1556–1608; tr. Frances E. Cox)[2]

Tuesday

The richest of poor men

St Francis (1181/2–1226), the son of a wealthy cloth merchant in northern Italy, is remembered for preaching to the birds and the wolf of Gubbio. He was undoubtedly a disturbing figure, who in the months after leaving home in 1205 wandered the forests and prayed in caves in the hills or in churches and crypts near Assisi. Looking unkempt and having lost weight, he begged for food and building materials. Some thought him insane, especially after he kissed a leper. However, he had heard God's call to repair God's house and had a desire to follow the example of Jesus and live in poverty. This became a joyful way of life for him and for those who came to join him. Francis found himself to be the richest of poor men because of the quality of relationships, clarity of thought and action and joyful simplicity poverty gave him.

In 2013, when Cardinal Jorge Mario Bergoglio was elected Pope, he took the name Francis after a fellow cardinal told him not to forget the poor. The name also signifies the environmental focus of his pontificate. Like St Francis, Pope Francis has held out new possibilities to a world threatened by its own success brought about through unsustainable materialism and consumerism. It is paradoxical that religious centres acquire wealth and power because people value and give to them, yet this wealth and power does not belong personally to any individual.

It is one of the gifts of those who commit to a religious life, along with vows of poverty, chastity and obedience, that they see things differently. They hold out to the rest of us the possibility of alternative lifestyles. Those who find such a lifestyle to be their vocation will learn that it requires commitment, imagination and hard work. However, others often comment on the fulfilment they sense in people who have chosen not to be defined by consumption and material success. We all need to ask: what is a good life? What makes us fulfilled and, in the deepest sense, happy?

The most frequently used measurement of a country's prosperity is gross domestic product (GDP). Per capita the UK ranks as one of the largest and most prosperous economies in the world. Ask whether we are the happiest society and we do much less well. Economic prosperity, it transpires, is not all that matters.

In 1972 the King of Bhutan, a small state in the Himalayan mountains, suggested that gross national happiness (GNH) is more important than GDP. He thought that sustainable development should be holistic and give equal importance to non-economic aspects of well-being. Bhutan's GNH index includes both traditional socio-economic concerns such as living standards, health and education, and less traditional aspects of culture and psychological well-being. It assesses the well-being of the Bhutanese population rather than making a subjective psychological ranking of 'happiness' alone.

Since 2002, there has been an annual World Happiness Report monitoring each country's performance in six categories: GDP per capita, social support, healthy life expectancy, freedom to make your own life choices, generosity of the general population, and perceptions of internal and external corruption levels. North European countries consistently perform well and the happiest countries are those where the gap between richest and poorest is least. In 2021, the UK ranked seventeenth.

What is becoming clear is that an overriding focus on narrow economic indications of success is damaging to one's well-being. It is a huge challenge to think and act differently. In the UK, the government commissioned *The Dasgupta Review* on the Economics of Biodiversity, which was published in 2021. This is a major contribution to recognizing that the economy is a wholly owned subsidiary of the environment. The main headlines of the review are:

- Our economies, livelihoods and well-being all depend on our most precious asset: nature.
- Our unsustainable engagement with nature is endangering the prosperity of current and future generations.
- At the heart of the problem lies deep-rooted, widespread institutional failure.
- We need to change how we think, act and measure success.

- We must ensure that our demands on nature do not exceed its supply, and that we increase nature's supply relative to its current level.
- We must change our measures of economic success to guide us on a more sustainable path.
- We have to transform our institutions and systems – in particular our finance and education systems – to enable these changes and sustain them for future generations.

Different ways of measuring a society's well-being will encourage us to think and act so that economic prosperity is not the only and not necessarily the main goal. They will force us to consider what we want for a good life and, in terms of wealth and consumption, to ask: what is enough?

In 1223, in the Italian hilltop town of Greccio, St Francis built what is remembered as the first Christmas crib. He said:

> I want to do something that will recall to the memory the little child who was born in Bethlehem and set before our bodily eyes in some way the inconveniences of his infant needs, how he lay in a manger, how with an ox and an ass standing by he lay upon the hay where he had been placed.
>
> In the crib at Greccio, simplicity was honoured, poverty was exalted, humility was commended and Greccio was made, as it were, a new Bethlehem.[3]

Put simply, love came down at Christmas and, in the end, love is what matters most to all of us.

When I was a young priest, I used to celebrate communion once a week for a small Franciscan community in Whitechapel in London's East End. I loved their lifestyle, but it took me a while to see how hard they had to work to maintain the joyful simplicity I found so attractive. Everything was rooted in prayer and a communal rule of life. Things worked because of their individual and communal thought, commitment, determination, time and energy. Such a spirituality can move mountains. It is the hope of the world.

'Tis the gift to be simple, 'tis the gift to be free,
'Tis the gift to come down where we ought to be,

And when we find ourselves in the place just right,
'Twill be in the valley of love and delight.
When true simplicity is gain'd,
To bow and to bend we will not be asham'd,
To turn, turn will be our delight,
Till by turning, turning we come round right.
(Anon., nineteenth century, American Shaker song, sung to tune of
    'Lord of the Dance')

Wednesday

Made in God's image

In the temple an unusual alliance of religious leaders tried to trap Jesus with a political question.

> 'Teacher, we know that you are sincere, and teach the way of God in accordance with truth, and show deference to no one; for you do not regard people with partiality. Tell us, then, what you think. Is it lawful to pay taxes to the emperor, or not?' But Jesus, aware of their malice, said, 'Why are you putting me to the test, you hypocrites? Show me the coin used for the tax.' And they brought him a denarius. Then he said to them, 'Whose head is this, and whose title?' They answered, 'The emperor's.' Then he said to them, 'Give therefore to the emperor the things that are the emperor's, and to God the things that are God's.'
> (Mt. 22.16–21)

Titian's biblical paintings were popular in sixteenth-century Venice. He was much sought after and must have been used to dealing with rich and powerful patrons. His life would have given him insight into capturing the dark dishonesty of the question being asked by religious leaders to trap Jesus, and in the painting *The Tribute Money*, Titian contrasts this with the openness of Jesus, as he looks the man in the eye and points his finger to God in heaven. The implication could not be clearer or more direct, and helps us read the Bible story right.

This passage is not about paying ordinary taxes, but the hated census – the poll tax levied on everyone by Rome. The freedom-fighters and activists would do anything to avoid paying it. Here lay the trap for Jesus: would he incite rebellion and civil disobedience?

They were in the temple, yet the hypocritical leaders had no problem digging out a coin. The image on the coin – and its inscription to 'Tiberius Caesar, son of God' – were a blasphemy, in the very temple! That's why Jesus told them not just to give it, but to *give back* this filthy abomination to Caesar where it belonged, and to give total allegiance to God in his temple.

This statement has been used sometimes to suggest we should obey the authorities in an even-handed balance with God. But Jesus totally rejected the claim by the human authority, Caesar, to usurp the image and place of God, and reminded them that everything belongs to God and is owed to God. Environmental activists know the dilemma well. Sometimes it may seem necessary to take direct action when the authorities usurp the place of God or are not making change quickly enough.

Whatever it says about God and Caesar, paying taxes and the Christian's engagement with political life, a Jew at the time of Jesus would have heard in this story an unspoken second question – one concerning what it means for us to be fully human: 'And you, whose image are you made in?' The directness of the answer in Titian's painting is clear. Knowing that we are made in God's image does not tell us what to do, but it is of great relevance to our call to live up to our best nature, to our spirit and our motivation.

In his depiction of the face of Jesus, Titian shows us a person who is also divine. Jesus' direct gaze and the touches of white on either side of his eyes transfigure his humanity. In the second century, St Irenaeus wrote in *Against Heresies* (4.20.7) that the unknowable God is found in creation and through his Son: 'For the glory of God is a living man; but the human life comes from [or, simply, is] the vision of God . . . the revelation of the Father which comes through the Word gives life to those who see God.' This is often popularized as 'the glory of God is a person fully alive' but it is Christ in whom God has become the 'living man', the fully alive human being, in whom we see God's glory. And it is by being in Christ that we find ourselves to be fully alive.

But we are a fickle people! We so easily give away the power that is clearly depicted by Titian as being in Christ.

A prayer written by one of my predecessors as Vicar of St Martin-in-the-Fields acknowledges the reality of our divided self, and our need of God's compassion if we are to know and heal ourselves and the suffering of the world. Recognizing our temptations, we must seek to find the *undivided* self in Christ, and thus the motivation and strength to face the challenges of the climate and environmental crises.

I am two people;
and one is longing to serve thee utterly, and one is afraid.
O Lord, have compassion upon me.

I am two people;
and one will labour to the end, and one is already weary.
O Lord, have compassion upon me.

I am two people;
And one knows the suffering of the world, and one knows only his
    own.
O Lord, have compassion upon me.

And may the Spirit of our Lord Jesus Christ
Fill my heart and the hearts of all people everywhere.
(Austen Williams, 1912–2001)

Thursday

Internationalism – the United Nations

The problems of climate change and the environment do not have national boundaries. Even with a strong sense of individual and national moral purpose, we need a collective international effort to combat global problems. It is difficult to achieve this level of integration and co-operation.

We are organized in nation states – geographical areas with their own histories, identities and political organization. We learn to love everywhere by first loving somewhere. Devotion to our own country, patriotism, is good when it teaches us to love our neighbours as ourselves. Sometimes rivalries develop that spill over into conflict. We know from bitter experience how costly this is. Of course, it is better for us and for the planet when people live and work together.

As an undergraduate theologian in the 1970s I was taught Christian Ethics by the late G. R. Dunstan. He stressed the importance of building institutions and conventions that support and sustain us and provide a basis for a common morality. In *The Artifice of Ethics*[4] Dunstan says that the institutions by means of which moral insights are embodied and carried forward include the criminal law and the Church. He worked closely with professional associations on their codes of ethics and disciplinary procedures, and he noted that a host of voluntary societies, such as Scouting and Guiding, Youth Hostelling and Voluntary Service Overseas, embody moral ideals and develop internal codes for the harmonious working of local communities and groups. None of these bodies is perfect, but they help protect us from our worst selves and sustain us as we move towards what Christians think of as God's kingdom and the way of peace and love.

Throughout the nineteenth century, international organizations were beginning to develop regulations and conventions to support human endeavour. For example, the International Red Cross and Red Crescent

Movement, which dates from the 1860s, provided recognition of medical services and care for the wounded on the battlefield, establishing the original Geneva Convention in 1864. The League of Nations was founded after the First World War. Its success was very limited but it led, after the Second World War, to the founding of the United Nations (UN), an intergovernmental organization to maintain international peace and security.

The UN exists to develop friendly relations among nations, to achieve international co-operation, and to be a centre for harmonizing the actions of nations for peace, dignity and equality on a healthy planet. The UN is also a forum in which it is possible for nations to speak critically with one another. It has developed organizations and programmes that address our global problems, such as the World Health Organization, the UN Refugee Agency, and the World Bank with its remit to unlock private finance for development and climate action. The UN is not loved by everyone and is perceived by some, particularly the richer countries that make the largest financial contributions to it, to be expensive and inefficient. The truth is that if we didn't have such an organization, we would need to invent one. Not only is the UN the best we have for the time being, it embodies and gives substance to our ideals of international collaboration.

The Intergovernmental Panel on Climate Change (IPCC) was founded in 1988 and is the UN body for assessing the science related to climate change. Through the contributions of hundreds of scientists around the world, it has produced six major assessments of the scientific basis of climate change, its impacts, future risks, and options for adaptation and mitigation, as well as reports on particular aspects of the science of climate change. Nations collectively need to reduce their planet-warming emissions 43 per cent by 2030 and stop adding carbon dioxide to the atmosphere altogether by the early 2050s. Current policies by governments are expected to reduce global emissions by only a few percentage points this decade. The world isn't becoming more energy efficient quickly enough to balance out continued growth in global economic activity. The science is clear, and we still just about have the time and the capacity to act in such a way as to meet the climate-change goals.

In 2015 the UN adopted the Sustainable Development Goals (SDGs), 17 interlinked global calls for action by all countries – poor, rich and middle income – to promote prosperity while protecting the planet. The SDGs recognize that addressing climate change and environmental degradation must go hand in hand with ending poverty, improving health and education, reducing inequality and developing economic growth. We will not make progress with climate change unless we make progress with all the goals. The aim agreed at the UN is that they are to be reached by 2030.

The pandemic has given an opportunity to look afresh at the urgency of doing things better. The question for each of us is whether we really want to.

In teaching his disciples to ask God for what they want when they pray, Jesus said:

'Ask, and it will be given to you; search, and you will find; knock, and the door will be opened for you. For everyone who asks receives, and everyone who searches finds, and for everyone who knocks, the door will be opened. Is there anyone among you who, if your child asks for bread, will give a stone? Or if the child asks for a fish, will give a snake? If you then, who are evil, know how to give good gifts to your children, how much more will your Father in heaven give good things to those who ask him!'
(Mt. 7.7–11)

Friday

Climate justice

The industrialized world has had the greatest benefits from the use of fossil fuels and it is the poor who carry the greatest burden of climate change. According to the IPCC report in April 2022, worldwide the richest 10 per cent of households are responsible for between a third to nearly half of all greenhouse gas emissions. The poorest 50 per cent of households contribute around 15 per cent of emissions. On the whole it is the richest people and wealthiest nations that are heating up the planet.

In 2006, the economist Nicholas Stern estimated that the impact of climate change would reduce gross domestic product globally by 5–20 per cent each year. He was criticized for over-stating the problem, but ten years later he said it had been an underestimate. International development agencies such as Christian Aid, Tearfund and CAFOD have made climate justice a priority precisely because the impact of climate change is so great, it undercuts much of the good economic development they are supporting.

What can seem rather abstract and theoretical becomes more understandable when it is personalized, and the development agencies appreciate this. Christian Aid has spoken of Jessica in Zimbabwe, who lost crops to drought; Villa in Haiti, who shelters people whose homes have been damaged in yet another hurricane, and, in Kenya, of the disruption caused by a road being destroyed by a flash flood. Climate change has an impact on quality of life, health and mortality. The effects are so great that the temptation is for poorer countries to imitate the richer ones and use fossil fuels to catch up in terms of economic development. However, that will compound the problems for the world as a whole. What is needed is climate finance for mitigation, adaptation to the climate crisis, and support for a just transition to clean energy.

At the Paris COP in 2015, one of the key decisions related to the contributions of rich countries to climate finance. Much was promised; little has been paid. The agreement in Glasgow requires rich countries to 'at least double' funds for adaptation to the climate crisis. Words are easy! However, there was no progress in getting developed countries to fulfil their promise to provide $100 billion a year in climate finance overall. Poorer countries are calling for new 'loss and damage' finance, but the Glasgow agreement only provides for a 'dialogue' to discuss 'arrangements'. A campaign has thus begun for a 'loss and damage' fund to compensate those hardest hit by losses and damages due to climate change.

In the economic crisis following the pandemic, the UK chose to reduce its expenditure on overseas aid from 0.7 per cent of GDP to 0.5 per cent. Aid was presented as a charitable cost we could no longer afford, at least until the economy picked up again. Many Christians found this unpalatable. Aid is not charity. It recognizes our connectedness and mutual obligations. In the face of global problems, we have to find a fair way to help those in greatest need, especially when the benefits we have received have to some extent been at the expense of others. Overseas aid often supports the UK's foreign policy and trade objectives. It is not charity so much as a matter of enlightened self-interest. It is good for us as well as those to whom we give. We ought to be proud of all that is done with our contribution.

Climate justice is also an issue within countries. In the UK, disadvantaged communities are likely to be the most affected by the impact of climate change and least able to withstand its effects. This is frequently illustrated in our news bulletins in relation to extreme weather and pollution, but the increase in cost of living – and particularly increased energy costs – has heightened the problem.

Loving our neighbour and fairness are obvious heartland issues for Christians. What is much more challenging is featuring these in public policy. One creative response is a free web tool called 'Climate Just',[5] for public service providers to:

- identify who is vulnerable to climate change and fuel poverty and why;
- highlight neighbourhoods where climate disadvantage is highest;
- explain the factors involved and help you to decide what actions to take.

Anyone can use the web tool to gain information and understanding. It gives very specific information about localities. Indeed, if you have access to the web, see what you can find out about your home area. Take a look at other places you know and learn what you can about the different vulnerabilities we face.

St Martin-in-the-Fields' Prayer for the World
O God, our heavenly Father,
give us a vision of our world as your love would make it:
a world where the weak are protected and none go hungry or poor;
a world where the benefits of civilized life are shared, and everyone
  can enjoy them;
a world where different races, nations and cultures live in tolerance
  and mutual respect;
a world where peace is built with justice, and justice is guided by love;
and give us the inspiration and courage to build it,
through Jesus Christ our Lord. Amen.
(Geoffrey Brown, 1930–2015, and John Pridmore, b. 1930)

Saturday

An everlasting voice

John Constable moved his family to Brighton in 1824, as Maria began to suffer from tuberculosis. The sea air was thought to be better for her. Constable himself continued to work in London most of the time, visiting the family for short periods of relaxation. He wasn't much struck with Brighton, at least to start with, and wrote to his friend Archdeacon John Fisher:

I am living here but I dislike the place . . . Brighton is the receptacle of the fashion and offscouring of London. The magnificence of the sea and its (to use your beautiful expression) everlasting voice is drowned in the din and lost in the tumult of stagecoaches, gigs, flys, etc – and the beach is Piccadilly (that part of it where we dined) by the sea-side. Ladies dressed and *undressed* – gentlemen in morning gowns and slippers on, or without them altogether about *knee deep* in the breakers – footmen, children, nursery maids, dogs, boys, fishermen, preventative service men with hangers and pistols, rotten fish and those hideous amphibious animals the old bathing women, whose language both in oaths and voice resembles men – are all mixed up together in endless and indecent confusion.[6]

Constable liked the more genteel part of Brighton's Marine Parade and the elegance of the long Chain Pier, though declared there was nothing in the town for the painter. However, he still filled his sketchbooks and admired the magnificence of the sea, the breakers and the sky, 'which have been lovely indeed and always varying'. He said the seabirds 'add to the wildness and to the sentiment of melancholy always attendant on the ocean'. In this seascape study, the boat with the red sail is roaring along and the storm is still some way off, but we can see it advancing at full force. Storms provide metaphors for life, and Maria died in the November after this sketch. Constable was watching the tragedy coming.

The sea connects us globally. Trade routes extend our horizons and provide goods we do not have in our part of the world. Shipping is a relatively efficient form of transport but contributes about 2.5 per cent of the world's CO_2, roughly equivalent to that produced by Germany, as well as a substantial quantity of other greenhouse gases. As with aviation, it seems strange that international agreement means maritime diesel is tax-exempt. People who go on cruises often comment on the recommendation that passengers give a large specified tip for staff. It is an admission that this is a poorly paid and under-regulated sector. In March 2022, there was a scandal in the UK when P&O ferries laid off 800 staff and hired new workers, many from other parts of the world, on lower wages. The maritime sector is working to be net zero by 2050, but it is one for which nations find it hard to legislate.

In recent years, we have become aware of people who have travelled long distances, sometimes in the very unsafe hands of people traffickers, seeking safety by crossing the English Channel. In 2021, 28,000 migrants crossed in small boats. At least 44 drowned or went missing. One can only imagine they believed the risks preferable to the danger they faced wherever they came from.

Taking control of our borders and reducing the number of migrants making such perilous journeys is easier said than done. Events in Hong Kong and Ukraine have a great impact. We live locally and globally, and the intersection is complex. Climate change has added to the number of migrants from places where life has become impossible, and globally there are more refugees on the move than at any time since the Second World War. Most of those who come are courageous, highly motivated and want to make a contribution in the UK. We are still working out how to respond positively.

We have been polluting the sea for centuries. Now we're using it as a rubbish dump for the 8 million metric tons of plastic that go into the world's oceans every year. In addition to the debris we see along the shoreline, there is now so much rubbish in the sea that it has formed five giant garbage patches. The largest — the Great Pacific Garbage Patch — includes an estimated 1.8

trillion pieces of rubbish and covers an area twice the size of France. Wave action and exposure to the sun breaks some of this into microplastics, and a certain quantity enters the food chain. Left alone it will take 400 years for most of the plastic to degrade and release chemicals, and these will further contaminate the sea.

Viewed from the land, the sea is a mysterious, only partly seen world. It is both beautiful and frightening. Even in a busy resort, walking along the shore has biblical resonances of creation and chaos, of call and discipleship, of storms at sea and of our learning to trust God through tempestuous dangers. We feel the power of the ocean in its wind, waves and tides.

Eight miles offshore from Brighton is a wind farm. At present it covers an area a little larger than Guernsey and generates nearly 1,400 gigawatt hours of electricity a year, enough to power nearly 350,000 homes, which is roughly half of Sussex. Wind turbines also generate controversy, but as we look out to sea they can take us towards new horizons and they renew my hope that we are finding a sustainable way to live. Wind turbines are not so much paradise regained and innocence restored as hopeful signs of the creative toil needed for us to live east of Eden.

At the edge of the land, by the sea, humanity is confronted by a different timescale. Here we hear the everlasting voice of God calling us to live not just for ourselves but for the good of all creation.

Dear Lord and Father of mankind,
Forgive our foolish ways;
Reclothe us in our rightful mind,
In purer lives thy service find,
In deeper reverence, praise.
(John Greenleaf Whittier, 1872)

Questions for Week 3

- What struck you from the material this week?
- What does it feel like to you to live 'east of Eden'? Are there particular challenges you fear or relish?
- What does it take for you to be happy? How do you feel personal happiness relates to the purpose of life?
- What would it mean for you and for others to have enough?

WEEK 4

Each lamp be bright
With ready light
To grace the marriage feast tonight.

Advent 4

What can I bring him?

Matthew's Gospel tells of the birth of Jesus the Messiah to the Virgin Mary, who was engaged to Joseph who was of David's line. This was the fulfilment of a prophecy, and the birth in Bethlehem needed no other explanation. There is no mention of a Roman census to explain why the family had left Nazareth, or the lack of a room at the inn, or visiting shepherds. Those are all in Luke's Gospel, while Mark begins with John the Baptist baptizing the adult Jesus, and John sets the whole story within the creation: 'In the beginning was the Word.' Only in Matthew do we hear of Magi from the East (probably modern-day Iran), more magical and mysterious than the translation 'wise men' implies. They had seen a star telling of a child born to be king of the Jews. They went to seek him in Jerusalem and were directed to Bethlehem by a scheming King Herod.

For Matthew, the Magi signalled that salvation for the world came from the Jews and the birth of this child had implications for earthly powers. Not until Tertullian in the second century did anyone identify the Magi as kings, and no one numbered them as only three, calling them Caspar, Melchior and Balthazar, until the ninth century, when these kings came to represent the known world of Europe, Africa and Asia. It was the English monk Bede who in the seventh century saw the symbolism of their gifts as offerings of gold for a king, incense for God, and myrrh for a human being who would, in dying, show us who God is with us.

Gossaert's painting was an altarpiece in front of which Mass was celebrated. It is fantastically detailed, rich and complex. In the ruins of the old dispensation, the beautifully dressed kings have come to worship the infant Christ, who is sitting on his mother's lap, very upright, and blessing what looks like a eucharistic vessel. Mary is lovingly serene, but Joseph is fearfully anxious. He is looking up to a stone frieze depicting the sacrifice of Isaac, whose father Abraham was prepared to sacrifice his son out of obedience to God. Joseph has a sense of what is coming.

Dogs are often depicted as faithful companions, but here in the foreground there is one gnawing a bone, a reminder of our mortality. In the corridor receding into the painting is a donkey and an open gate to a way that leads to the city, Jerusalem. In the night sky, angels announce a new dawn. Onlookers have gathered, and there is a hardly visible self-portrait of the artist, looking in through the gap to the right of Joseph. This is the gospel in one view – and it is for everyone.

In this last week of Advent our focus is on what we can do to counter climate change and environmental destruction. Our gifts this Christmas could be small acts of doing things differently that give light and hope.

What can I give him, poor as I am?
If I were a shepherd, I would bring a lamb;
If I were a wise man, I would do my part;
Yet what I can I give him: give my heart.
(Christina Georgina Rossetti, *c.* 1872)

Monday

Gold – money

If you want to know what a person believes, ask what they spend their money on. In the nativity, gold is the gift for a king and, like all gifts, it can be used for good and ill.

In March 2022, the *Financial Times* reported the analysis of a coalition of campaign groups organized by the Rainforest Action Network (which builds partnerships with local, indigenous and frontline communities). In 2021, banks globally provided $742 billion in finance to coal, oil and gas companies, despite the climate pledges made by lenders to former Bank of England governor Mark Carney's net-zero banking alliance. The world's 60 largest lenders provided only slightly less financing for fossil fuels in 2021 than the $750 billion recorded in 2020. Since the Paris Agreement was signed in 2016, the banks have provided a total of $4.6 trillion, peaking in 2019 at $830 billion.

In the transition to renewable energy, there is an urgent need for green finance to have much greater priority. At present, it comprises a tiny proportion of loans and investments. Consumers can exercise considerable power by choosing good options when possible, but the big money is in the hands of investment managers. Most of us are not part of that world and cannot effect change through finance, but some of our money is managed corporately, for example in pension funds and in investments held by charities and churches.

By responding to the previous church reports, the work of the Ethical Investment Advisory Group (EIAG) and the encouraging debates of General Synod, the National Investing Bodies (NIBs) of the Church of England (the Church Commissioners, Church of England Pensions Board and funds managed by CCLA including the Central Board of Finance) are widely seen to be at the forefront of responsible investment. They gave an excellent report to General Synod in July 2021 on their approach to climate change.

They recognize the climate crisis is likely to affect every person, business and ecosystem, and that dramatic steps need to be taken to make the transition to a low-carbon economy. They have developed an active investment strategy that includes divestment from the most polluting companies, engagement with companies to ensure the alignment of those invested in fossil fuel with the Paris Agreement and a commitment to new sustainable investments. This approach has been informed with advice and support from the Ethical Investment Advisory Group and endorsed by General Synod. The NIBs are committed to achieving net-zero emissions portfolios by 2050 at the latest and making substantial progress to achieve net zero earlier.

The initial divestment from coal and tar sands, the fossil fuels with the worst impact on the environment, was modest in financial terms but powerfully symbolic and an indication of the willingness to divest. Engagement with companies has been a powerful tool for change, using the Church's moral authority and the benefits of getting together with a growing number of other investors seeking similar goals. Working with the Environment Agency and the Grantham Institute at the London School of Economics, we developed the Transition Pathway Initiative to track the transition of major carbon-intensive companies and inform investment decisions (see the Transition Pathway Initiative's website). In 2021, this was supported by 105 funds with $26 trillion in assets under management. The Transition Pathway continues to grow and become both more influential and powerful. Some activists still campaign for a more rigorous divestment from fossil fuels but, given our continued dependence on fossil fuels in at least the medium term, we can make a more sustained contribution through this policy of engagement. It has led to demonstrable changes in company actions by some of the world's largest corporations. In 2020, £32.2 million was divested by the NIBs from nine companies that failed to respond adequately to engagement and meet interim climate standards. This is adding pressure on others as we come to the 2023 review of the Church's investments.

Those who are wealthy enough to have investments increasingly want to ensure that their money is doing good. They and local charities and churches do not need to reinvent the wheel and can use the same responsible investment criteria developed by the Church of England. They are updated regularly and are easily available on the web by searching for the EIAG's policies and reviews. We all have a stake in these investments and our active engagement through General Synod helps to hold those who act for us to account.

Those of us who do not have personal financial investments still have economic power in the way we choose to use our money, offering a clear indication of what we believe. In an obvious extension of giving gifts at Christmas, many charities hold special appeals, including the church where I used to be Vicar, St Martin-in-the-Fields. Its Christmas Appeal began in 1927 on what is now BBC Radio 4. One year, on the Sunday of the broadcast, I answered the phone at a minute before 10 p.m. (when the lines were to close) after a very long day. The caller told me a long story of how, almost 30 years ago, the appeal had helped her when she was in desperate circumstances. She said that for the first time in her life she was able to give something back and made a gift of £10.

It is human to give. We can all do it in one way or another. And we can all take an active interest in the ways people look after our collective money – that held by the likes of churches, charities and pension funds with a responsibility for the common good.

Take my silver and my gold;
not a mite would I withhold.
Take my intellect and use
every power as thou shalt choose,
every power as thou shalt choose.
(Frances R. Havergal, 1874)

Tuesday

Frankincense – worship

Frankincense is for the worship of God, the smoke of incense rising to the heavens. Such worship is at the heart of the Christian Church, and it is important to get its relationship with morality the right way round, otherwise we lose vision and creativity, and become dull and moralistic. In *The Vision of God*,[1] Kenneth Kirk wrote that it is not that morality is the end of life and worship helps it, but that worship is the end of life and the way we behave is the test of it. In our prayers and worship, we offer thanks and praise for the gift of creation. We include the care of creation in the regular prayers, preaching and teaching of the Church. This integration is looked for in A Rocha's Eco Church awards which, as we have seen, are a structured way for a church to engage with the fifth Mark of Mission.

In response to the General Synod's aim for the Church of England to become net zero by 2030, we first had to agree a definition of what that means. Inevitably we have focused on our buildings, and if you look at the Church of England's environment programme web pages, you will find guidance on a practical path to net zero. There is a simple tool to measure your church building's carbon footprint and some helpful case studies. Insulation is particularly useful as a way of improving energy efficiency in a historic building. In some churches and associated buildings, it has been possible to install solar panels, but all of us can switch to a renewable energy supplier and use LED light bulbs. It helps to make a plan and to identify some person or group to be your environmental champion.

Decisions about heating often come as an emergency after an old system has broken down, but now the environmental impact of whatever replaces it must be considered. Inevitably we are moving away from oil and gas and looking for cleaner and greener solutions. There is no one solution that will work everywhere. New technology, rather than a straight replacement, might involve a higher capital expenditure but if it's a long-term investment it can be good value.

Education in these contexts informs the way we live, so the influence of what is done by the Church can be extensive. Churches, chaplaincies and schools have key roles within their communities. When a congregation thinks beyond the building, greater consideration is given to the ways in which we eat, heat our homes and care for our public spaces. We become more aware of the energy we use and how we can have an impact on the wider community. Good public transport does not exist everywhere. Travel in rural areas can be transformed with the development of community transport, shared cars, more bikes and cycle paths, safer roads and so on. All sorts of good things can develop for their communities from churches doing environmental things well.

When I was young, churches started to introduce Traidcraft coffee. It wasn't always popular but it got us thinking, talking and praying about trade justice and the power of the consumer. Now every supermarket is full of products with a variety of ethical marks. The variety is a bit confusing, but the supply is evidence that consumers want to buy what has been ethically sourced. We need to go through a similar process quickly in terms of environmental discussions, using our power to press for change. Creativity, resilience and recognizing the wisdom of old ways in our present circumstances can be a joy.

Religious faith is a powerful resource for this transition. Churches witness that there is more to life than materialistic consumerism, though it can be difficult to handle the tension that has grown between the way society celebrates Christmas through mass consumption and the change of lifestyle to which Christianity points.

The worldwide Church keeps a season of Creation from 1 September to 4 October, the Feast of St Francis. For those of us in the UK, this fits well with the celebration of the Harvest Festival. The Church of England's Liturgical Commission has helpfully produced *A Time of Creation: Liturgical Resources for Creation and the Environment*.[2] This recognizes the need to give thanks for the great gift of God's creation, to offer lament for its destruction, whether wilful or unthinking, and to pray that the natural environment may be protected and restored. Perhaps the challenge in this week leading up to Christmas is to ask how we mark the care of creation in the gifts brought to the infant Christ in the crib. How might the power of Christianity be used to address the issues of climate change and environmental degradation?

As I was writing this reflection, the RSPB published a report saying there are 600 million fewer birds in Europe than in 1980. That means we have lost 1 in 6 of the bird population. We also all know there is a problem with the loss of insects, especially pollinators. However, another recent report says that there are parts of the world where we have destroyed half the insect population. This is lamentable.

There are numerous gifts we could bring from the Church to the crib for God in Jesus to bless: projects, people and so many steps in the right direction. But the truth of whatever we are doing about climate change and the environment now is that we are in no position to be self-satisfied. It is both a brutal truth and a wake-up call that we have mucked up and need forgiveness and restoration. This Christmas I will come to the crib like the penitent thief beside the crucified Jesus, asking him to remember me when he comes into his kingdom. There are times, as we face climate-change and environmental crises, when I know God in Jesus Christ is our only hope. In the words of the hymn 'Rock of Ages':

Nothing in my hand I bring,
Simply to the cross I cling.
(A. M. Toplady, 1740–78)

Perhaps what we should do today is lament our indifference and our failures in relation to climate change and offer something good that we are involved in, or know about, for Christ to bless. When we get one thing right and do it well, other things tend to follow and we gain momentum in the right direction.

Yours, Lord, is the greatness, the power,
the glory, the splendour, and the majesty;
for everything in heaven and on earth is yours.
All things come from you,
and of your own do we give you.[3]

Wednesday

Myrrh – death and lifestyle

Myrrh is the gift from the Magi foretelling that the infant Jesus is going to die for love of God's world. The gospel begins, not in Bethlehem, but in the bewilderment of an empty tomb on Easter Day. What is born at the resurrection is eternal life in which we share. Death is not the last word. In the end, goodness is stronger than evil, love is stronger than hate, light is stronger than darkness, life is stronger than death. Our circumstances are serious but even we can't keep a good God down. That is our hope, and the death of Christ means that in our new life in him we are going to have to change our ways.

Food is a big thing at Christmas. Families and friends gather and a lot of churches organize meals for those who would otherwise be on their own. Many of us will be thinking about the feast to be prepared. Traditions vary but there is usually a lot of meat. Though we are celebrating a special occasion, most of us eat too much meat for the good of our own health and for the good of the planet. We need to move to a more plant-based diet. A quarter of greenhouse gases globally come from food and agriculture. If wealthier countries reduced their meat-rich diets, much less land would be needed to grow food, and vast areas could be rewilded, offering a double dividend.

A special meal in a group that is larger than usual gives opportunities to experiment. In my family, our children have a healthier and more environmentally friendly diet than I do. They cook in different ways from those I knew growing up. Have fun trying new things. A nut roast is now not just for the vegetarians and vegans. If you have a garden, enjoy growing some of your own produce. See if you can use food that is seasonal and local, so reducing transport costs.

About a third of the world's food goes to waste. Producing, transporting and letting food rot releases 8–10 per cent of global greenhouse gases.

According to the UN's Food and Agriculture Organization, if food waste were a country it would have the third largest carbon footprint after the USA and China. At Christmas we plan meals carefully, but we also need to plan to reduce waste and be creative with leftovers. Rather than throw food away, we can turn ripe fruit into sweet smoothies, or bake with it or make jams. Just by talking about the issue of food waste, we help people become more aware of the problem and seek ways to address it. There are some great food projects across the country, many of them using food that would otherwise go to waste to feed people on benefits or without recourse to benefits. Find out what is going on locally. They will be grateful for volunteers throughout the year.

The mantra 'Reduce, Reuse, Recycle' is a helpful way of thinking about what we can do personally. There are plenty of online tips for individuals and households who want to support the global effort to tackle and adapt to climate change. For example, the UK Climate Change Committee suggests the following.

The way you travel
- Choose to walk and cycle or take public transport in preference to a car.
- Make your next car an electric one, and then charge it 'smartly'.
- Minimise flying, especially long-haul, where possible.

In your home
- Improve the energy efficiency of your home (or ask your landlord to) through draughtproofing, improved insulation, choosing LED light-bulbs and appliances with high efficiency ratings.
- Set thermostats no higher than 19°C and the water temperature in heating systems no higher than 55°.
- Consider switching to a low-carbon heating system such as a heat pump, especially if you live off the gas grid; if you are on the gas grid consider a hybrid system.
- Reduce the risk of overheating in the summer by opting for thick curtains or blinds.
- Install water and smart energy meters to manage water and energy use, whilst also helping to identify water leaks.

What you eat and buy
- Eat a healthy diet, for example with less beef, lamb and dairy.
- Eliminate food waste as far as possible and make sure that you use separate food waste collections if available. Reduce, reuse and recycle your other waste too.
- Use only peat-free compost.
- Choose good quality products that will last, use them for longer and try to repair before you replace.
- Share rather than buy items like power tools that you don't use frequently. If you don't/won't use your car regularly then consider joining a car club instead.

What else?
- Look for changes that you can make in your workplace or school to reduce emissions and support your colleagues to make changes too.
- If you're in a flood risk area sign up to flood warnings and devise your own household plan to prepare for possible floods.
- Talk about your experiences and help to raise awareness of the need to act. Consider the wider impacts of your actions (e.g. through your pension or ISA and via the companies you buy from).[4]

The list may seem a bit bland, but it is a good start for discussion and for personal action planning. For example, second-hand clothes from relatives, friends and charity shops and wearing them for longer makes better use of them, and reduces waste and our carbon footprint. These lifestyle changes imply too that we need a different relationship with time: we should slow down and pause more often.

Make a plan of what you will do to reduce your carbon footprint: think and pray, plan, act, review. See if you can make this a continuous process.

Religion inspires and motivates us. For Christians the kingdom of God is a vision of how life can be.

A vision without a task is but a dream.
A task without a vision is drudgery.
A vision and a task is the hope of the world.[5]

Thursday

'Awake, Jerusalem, awake!'

The Magi did not return to Jerusalem, because they had been warned in a dream to return home by another route. They knew the limits and the dangers of political power. In this last week of Advent, we are focusing on what we can do personally in response to climate change and the environment. It may seem a bit odd to return to Westminster, the UK's centre of political power, but we live in a democracy and each of us has a part to play in the political process, so return we must.

I love Monet's painting *The Thames below Westminster*. Both of the parishes in which I served as Vicar border the Thames. The parish of St Martin-in-the-Fields comes down to the river close to the place from which Monet was viewing Westminster. It is easy to enjoy the image just as it is, but what the artist was depicting was the political centre of a city in which there had been massive visionary change. During his first stay in London, Monet was captivated by London's fog, saying: 'Without the fog, London would not be a beautiful city. It's the fog that gives it its magnificent breadth.'

I grew up in north London and remember the 'pea souper' smog of 4–7 December 1962 when we could see so little that I walked into a lamp post on my way to school. It was eerily quiet and the smell of sulphur was in the air. People who could get them wore masks, as we have done during the pandemic, but most of us simply had to cover our nose and mouth with a scarf or handkerchief. This was eight years after the Clean Air Act of 1956, which restricted burning coal at home and introduced smokeless zones. In 1962, 700 people died because of the London smog. In 1952 it had been 12,000. It takes time to make a difference, but we succeeded in changing the way we lived in order to get clean air and water, and improve the environment.

Monet's misty composition is anchored by carefully positioned structures – the horizontal jetty in the foreground, with Westminster Bridge marking the horizon, and the vertical Houses of Parliament. Every architectural element in the picture was new at the time. The Victoria Embankment on the right had just been completed. Built out into the river, it provided a modern sewerage system, while the road relieved congestion from Trafalgar Square along the Strand and Fleet Street. Charles Barry's iconic Houses of Parliament had also just been finished, ten years after the architect's death. The exaggerated height of the towers increases its significance. St Thomas' Hospital, the low rectangular shape on the far left, was also nearing completion before opening in the summer of 1871. Westminster Bridge had been reconstructed in 1862. Even in fog, this city had energy, vision and purpose.

Today, fog is rare but, like every city, London has problems with air quality and pollution. Being by the river helps, as does congestion charging, the Ultra Low Emission Zone and the greater use of public transport, bicycles and walking. The Houses of Parliament are now in a poor state of repair: the building is crumbling and needs major restoration and renewal at a cost estimated between £7 billion and £22 billion and a timescale of up to 76 years. By contrast, the Scottish Parliament Building cost £414 million and was much criticized for going over budget. The Senedd Cymru, Welsh Parliament, was built for an also much criticized £70 million.

Barry's building gives a strong account of what Parliament is: a two-party oppositional democracy with an understanding of Magna Carta built in, with the king or queen and their government under the law. Religion and the bishops take their part in holding the Crown and the government to account. Prayers are said at the beginning of every day, including this prayer, which sets out a very clear hope of what Parliament is about:

Almighty God, by whom alone Kings reign, and Princes decree justice; and from whom alone cometh all counsel, wisdom, and understanding; we thine unworthy servants, here gathered together in thy Name, do most humbly beseech thee to send down thy Heavenly Wisdom from above, to direct and guide us in all our consultations; and grant that, we having thy fear always before our eyes, and laying aside all private interests, prejudices, and partial affections, the result of all our counsels may be to the glory of thy blessed Name, the maintenance of true Religion and Justice, the safety, honour, and happiness of the Queen, the publick wealth, peace and tranquillity of the Realm, and the uniting and knitting together of the hearts of all persons and estates within the same, in true Christian Love and Charity one towards another, through Jesus Christ our Lord and Saviour. Amen.[6]

In its architecture, Parliament has clear purpose but the building is now down at heel, the manner of voting is archaic, there is a poor phone signal and weak wi-fi. It feels like a metaphor for a crumbling democracy and an increasingly divided United Kingdom as we move towards the end of a remarkable Elizabethan era. In preparation for its restoration and renewal, there has been an absence of discussion about the nature of a parliamentary democracy that will serve not the mid-nineteenth but the mid- to late-twenty-first century and beyond. The discussion has been limited to restoration of the building, a technological upgrade of services and improvement to access. How will we use what we have learned during the pandemic about the effectiveness of online meetings and, in relation to climate change in particular, a more participatory democracy through the very successful and creative citizens' assembly in Birmingham convened by Parliament?

In a speech at the time of COP26 in Glasgow, Greta Thunberg said that our leaders were not leading. As a campaigning slogan it's not entirely fair, for many parliamentarians are environmental champions, and the UK has been at the forefront of environmental legislation. We do need, however, to make sure we continue to be so in our new circumstances outside the EU. The UK Climate Change Committee's work is outstanding, but there is a strong feeling among environmentalists that our political processes are not adequate.

The Magi did not return to Jerusalem, but we need to. The renewal of our parliamentary building is an opportunity for so much more than its historic restoration. It is an opportunity to renew democracy.

Where there is no vision, the people perish: but he that keepeth the law, happy is he.
(Prov. 29.18, KJV)

Friday

Plant a tree

There is more to trees than meets the eye. The sizeable root systems underground anchor and nourish them but also form a communications network that is only just beginning to be understood. For us, trees provide environmental and social benefits, including capturing and storing carbon dioxide. They improve biodiversity, stabilize soil erosion and reduce flood risk. Currently, around 13 per cent of the UK is covered by woodland. In England, the figure is 10 per cent, much lower than in other European countries such as France (32 per cent), Germany (33 per cent) and Spain (37 per cent). The UK government's aim is to increase forestry cover to 17 per cent by 2050. To do this, we need to plant 30,000 hectares of woodland every year – more than 90 million trees. Scotland is doing well, while England is not yet planting even a third of its target. Wales has done even less, which may be why the Welsh government has committed to giving every household a tree to plant. Joyfully, tree-planting for the Queen's Platinum Jubilee was an initiative across the Commonwealth.

In 2015, as preparation for the Paris Climate Change summit, I went with Christian Aid to Malawi to see the impact of climate change there. There had been destructive floods earlier in the year and there was drought when I went. Farmers said they used to know when the rains would come but that was no longer true. The last project we visited was a small group who looked to be the poorest people we met that week. They had planted fruit trees to prevent soil erosion. Their trees would not fruit for four or five years, so what they had done was an act of faith, and they were guarding the trees with their lives. I felt ashamed that I was not making anything like as much effort to guard God's gift of creation, and came home determined to do more.

At a lovely celebration in December 2021 to mark the centenary of Hilfield Friary in Dorset, the Anglican Society of Saint Francis planted 100 trees. In the service sheet, it said:

Our planting of trees today is a sign of harmony between us and creation and a sign of hope in a greener future, of habitable space for future generations to come.

May the Lord bless these trees, so that they may have good roots to keep the soil from eroding and many leaves and branches to provide homes for the birds of the air, the many insects, our brothers and sisters, and so that we may have fresh air to breathe.

In 2022, the National Trust reported an 80 per cent decline in the number of small orchards in England and Wales since 1900. This equates to losing an area almost twice the size of Bristol and is particularly significant for flora and fauna. Tree-planting needs our help.

Martin Luther said that even if he knew the world would go to pieces tomorrow, he would still plant an apple tree. Planting a tree is one of the most hopeful things any of us can do in the face of adversity, and few actions have given me more pleasure than doing this myself, or having someone plant a tree in my name. Of course, it is important to seek good advice and plant the right tree in the right place.

You might want to think about what other hopeful actions you can take, but if you are still looking for a last-minute Christmas present, you can buy a tree online from organizations such as the Woodland Trust, the National Trust and the National Forest. They provide a certificate for you to give the person receiving the gift of a tree, to tell them it has been done in their name. A tree links Christmas to the crucifixion on Good Friday.

> Behold the wood of the cross on which was hung the saviour of the world.
> Come, let us worship.
> (Ancient Liturgy for Good Friday)

It is a sign of our redemption and would make a very happy Christmas present. Getting serious about climate change is not pain free but it is hopeful:

> For you shall go out in joy,
> and be led back in peace;

the mountains and the hills before you
    shall burst into song,
    and all the trees of the field shall clap their hands.
Instead of the thorn shall come up the cypress;
    instead of the brier shall come up the myrtle;
and it shall be to the Lord for a memorial,
    for an everlasting sign that shall not be cut off.
(Is. 55.12–13)

Saturday

Christmas Eve – Jesus Christ the apple tree

Advent brings us to Christmas, and Luther's assertive hope of planting an apple tree, even in a crisis, suggested to me that Crivelli's extraordinarily beautiful painting, *Madonna of the Candle*, would work well as an end and as a new beginning. The Virgin and child are set in a nourishing abundance of fruit, a reminder of the garden of Eden and of the fall being redeemed by the incarnation. The Madonna is crowned and enthroned. This is how things can and will be in the new Jerusalem, the kingdom of heaven. There are apples aplenty, including one placed as an offering on the step, but what the infant Christ is holding is a pear! It may be fanciful but I would like to think this is about both the fruitfulness of Christ and the idea that redemption isn't repetition but takes us somewhere new, with a great variety of goodness.

Like so many religious paintings now in art galleries, this was a panel from an altarpiece. Its surrounding panels have been scattered to Venice, Florence, Lille and Denver, as well as the Pinacoteca di Brera in Milan. Thus the elements of the altarpiece can only be seen out of context, in secular space, rather than as one in the cathedral in Camerino, from where Crivelli's work was rescued after the devastating earthquake that destroyed the cathedral in 1799. This is one of the religious problems of our age and it has come up for us several times in the pages of this book. Many scientists and politicians know the importance of faith in helping the world face the existential crises of climate change and the environment. Paintings such as this still have an effect in the wider secular world, which treasures them and exhibits them for our enjoyment and learning, but faith will only nourish the world and fully play its part when earthed in the context of worship and a community.

Crivelli was a master of illusion and perspective. The painting is three-dimensional with depth and a foreground that leads into our space. We stand before it as we would before an altar, offering gifts of fruit and flowers and a candle – the symbols of our prayers for what we most desire. At Christmas, many of us glimpse the possibility and hope of God come among us in Jesus Christ and of our humanity and broken world being remade.

The image of Jesus Christ the apple tree has its roots in a beautiful passage from the Song of Solomon:

> As an apple tree among the trees of the wood,
>   so is my beloved among young men.
> With great delight I sat in his shadow,
>   and his fruit was sweet to my taste.
> He brought me to the banqueting house,
>   and his intention towards me was love.
> Sustain me with raisins,
>   refresh me with apples;
>   for I am faint with love.
> O that his left hand were under my head,
>   and that his right hand embraced me!
> I adjure you, O daughters of Jerusalem,
>   by the gazelles or the wild does:
> do not stir up or awaken love
>   until it is ready!
> (Song of Sol. 2.3–7)

The image is used too in a carol best known now to music by Elizabeth Poston. As with so much at Christmas, there is two-way traffic between the religious and the secular, and the Christmas Eve secular observance of the old English winter tradition of wassailing, or wishing health to apple trees, a celebration involving a good deal of cider. In any case, it makes for a celebratory end to our Advent, for there is much to enjoy in God's good creation and in its redemption by our Lord Jesus Christ.

> The tree of life my soul hath seen,
> Laden with fruit and always green;
> The trees of nature fruitless be,
> Compared with Christ the apple tree.

His beauty doth all things excel,
By faith I know but ne'er can tell
The glory which I now can see,
In Jesus Christ the apple tree.

For happiness I long have sought,
And pleasure dearly I have bought;
I missed of all but now I see
'Tis found in Christ the apple tree.

I'm weary with my former toil –
Here I will sit and rest awhile,
Under the shadow I will be,
Of Jesus Christ the apple tree.

I'll sit and eat this fruit divine,
It cheers my heart like spirit'al wine;
And now this fruit is sweet to me,
That grows on Christ the apple tree.

This fruit doth make my soul to thrive,
It keeps my dying faith alive;
Which makes my soul in haste to be
With Jesus Christ the apple tree.
(Eighteenth-century carol)

Questions for Week 4

- What struck you from the material this week?
- What gift will you offer at the crib this Christmas in response to what you have been reading, thinking and praying about through Advent?
- What do you want to say to your representatives in Parliament, on the local council and in church?
- What will you do differently in response to climate change and environmental crises?

Christmas Day

Happy Christmas!

Welcome, all wonders in one sight!
   Eternity shut in a span;
Summer in winter; day in night;
   Heaven in earth, and God in man.
Great little one, whose all-embracing birth
Lifts earth to heaven, stoops heav'n to earth.
(Richard Crashaw, c. 1613–49)

And finally . . .

If you want to find out more, there is a huge amount of information out there. These websites and books are helpful, but this is no more than my idiosyncratic list to help get you to go further.

Some useful websites

Church

A Rocha, <https://arocha.org.uk/about-us/>

Caring for God's Acre,

Church Investors Group, <https://churchinvestorsgroup.org.uk>

Church of England Environment Programme,
    <www.churchofengland.org/about/environment-and-climate-change>

Church of England Ethical Investment Advisory Group, Policies and Reviews,
    <www.churchofengland.org/about/leadership-and-governance/ethical-investment-advisory-group/policies-and-reviews>.

Faith for the Climate, <https://faithfortheclimate.org.uk>

Hope for the Future, <www.hftf.org.uk>

Laudato Si' Research Institute, Campion Hall Oxford,
    <https://lsri.campion.ox.ac.uk/>

Operation Noah, <https://operationnoah.org/>

Christian Development charities for whom climate justice is a priority

Catholic Agency for Overseas Development, <https://cafod.org.uk/>

Christian Aid,

Tearfund, <www.tearfund.org/about-us/our-team>

Information, analysis, policy

Carbon Brief,

The Conservation Foundation, <https://conservationfoundation.co.uk/>
Environment and Climate Intelligence Unit, <https://eciu.net>
Feedback, <https://feedbackglobal.org/about-us>
Intergovernmental Panel on Climate Change,
Rapid Transition Alliance,
Transition Pathway Initiative,
UK Parliament Climate Change Committee,
United Nations, <www.un.org/en/>

Books

Church statements

Just about every denomination has published policy and position papers. Two
of the best:
Church of Sweden, *A Bishops' Letter about the Climate*, 2014.
Pope Francis, *Laudato si'*, 2015.

Information, analysis, policy

This is constantly changing, so the websites are usually more helpful. I found
these books particularly useful. Black is a former BBC journalist who set
up the reliable Environment and Climate Intelligence Unit (I was on their
Advisory Board). His book destroys the false myths about climate change
still sometimes used in public debate. Klein is wonderfully provocative,
integrated and influential. She published in the run-up to the Paris COP21.
Rapley is a distinguished climate scientist who wrote and performed a play
as a way of communicating what the future might bring.

Richard Black, *Denied: The Rise and Fall of Climate Contrarianism*, The Real
Press, 2018.
Naomi Klein, *This Changes Everything: Capitalism vs the Climate*, Penguin
Random House, 2014.
Chris Rapley and Duncan Macmillan, *2071: The World We'll Leave Our
Grandchildren*, John Murray, 2015.

Theology and spirituality

There are lots, so these are varied tasters.

Church of England, *A Time for Creation: Liturgical Resources for Creation and the Environment*, Church House Publishing, 2020.

Simon Cocksedge, Samuel Double and Nicholas Alan Worssam, *Seeing Differently: Franciscans and Creation*, Canterbury Press, 2021.

Thich Nhat Hanh, *A Love Letter to the Earth*, Parallax Press, 2013.

Martin Hodson and Margot R. Hodson, *A Christian Guide to Environmental Issues*, Bible Reading Fellowship, 2021.

Nathan Levy, David Shreeve and Harriman Haleem, *Sharing Eden: Green Teachings from Jews, Christians and Muslims*, Kube Publishing and The Conservation Foundation, 2012.

Michael P. Nelson and Kathleen Dean Moore (eds), *Moral Ground: Ethical Action for a Planet in Peril* (TX: Trinity University Press, 2010), with a Foreword by Archbishop Desmond Tutu and contributions from 80 leaders, including Gus Speth, whose quote was one of my starting points.

Ruth Valerio, *Saying Yes to Life*, SPCK, 2020.

Wonderfully practical

Not that the rest aren't, but these are in a class of their own.

Nancy Birtwhistle, *Clean and Green: 101 Hints and Tips for a More Eco-friendly Home*, One Boat, 2021.

Claire Foster and David Shreeve, *Don't Stop at the Lights: Leading Your Church Through a Changing Climate*, Church House Publishing, 2008.

Notes

Introduction

1 It is available, along with EIAG's other policies, on the Church of England website at: <www.churchofengland.org/about/leadership-and-governance/ethical-investment-advisory-group/policies-and-reviews>.

2 This has been much quoted and the ideas can be found in his writings and broadcasts, for example: James Gustafson Speth, *The Bridge at the End of the World: Capitalism, the Environment and Crossing from Crisis to Sustainability* (New Haven, CT: Yale University Press, 2008) and 'Shared Planet, Religion and Nature', BBC Radio 4, 1 October 2013.

3 Collect for the First Sunday of Advent, *Common Worship: Daily Prayer* (London: Archbishops' Council/Church House Publishing, 2005).

Week 1

1 IPCC Special Report, *Global Warming of 1.5 °C*, 2019, available at: <www.ipcc.ch/sr15/>.

2 Sir Robert Watson, Chair of the Intergovernmental Science-Policy Platform on Biodiversity and Ecosystem Services (IPBES), 6 May 2020.

3 Encyclical Letter *Laudato si'* of the Holy Father Francis on Care for Our Common Home, 2015, paras 1–2, available at: <https://cafod.org.uk/content/download/25373/182331/file/papa-francesco_20150524_enciclica-laudato-si_en.pdf>.

4 Pope Francis, General Audience, 16 September 2020, Vatican Media.

5 The letters can be read in full at: <https://creationtide.wordpress.com/letters-for-creation/>.

6 Copyright © Geoffrey Gardner. Available at: <www.godsongs.net/2020/10/from-the-tiny-ant-to-the-elephant.html>.

Week 2

1 For the full quote see 'Great Works of Western Art – Salisbury Cathedral from the Bishop's Garden', available at: <worldsbestpaintings.net>.

2 See: <www.edenproject.com/mission>.

3 *Common Worship: Services and Prayers for the Church of England* (London: Archbishops' Council/Church House Publishing, 2000).

4 *Common Worship: Services and Prayers.*
5 Thomas Traherne, *Centuries of Meditations*, 28, available at: <https://ccel.org/ccel/t/traherne/centuries/cache/centuries.pdf>.
6 The Magnificat, from Evening Prayer, the Book of Common Prayer.
7 Rowan Williams, *The Poems of Rowan Williams* (Oxford: Perpetua Press, 2002).
8 See: <aa.org/the-twelve-steps>.
9 A prayer based on words from Dag Hammarskjöld (1905–61), United Nations Secretary-General, published posthumously in Sweden in 1963 in *Vägmärken* and in English as *Markings*, translated by Leif Sjöberg and W. H. Auden, 1964.
10 Julian of Norwich, *Revelations of Divine Love*, ch. 5.

Week 3

1 Alison Latham (ed.), *The Oxford Companion to Music* (Oxford: OUP, 2002).
2 J. S. Bach, Cantata BWV 140.
3 Drawn from the writings of St Francis's first biographer, Thomas of Celano.
4 G. R. Dunstan, *The Artifice of Ethics* (London: SCM, 1974).
5 This web tool has been developed by Climate UK, Joseph Rowntree, Environment Agency and the University of Manchester; available at: <https://www.climatejust.org.uk/welcome-climate-just-web-tool>.
6 James Hamilton, *Constable: A Portrait* (London: Weidenfeld & Nicolson, 2022), p. 263.

Week 4

1 K. E. Kirk, *The Vision of God* (Cambridge: James Clarke and Co Ltd, 1931).
2 The Church of England, *A Time For Creation: Liturgical Resources for Creation and the Environment* (London: Church House Publishing, 2020).
3 Prayer at the Preparation of the Table (based on 1 Chron. 29.11–13), *Common Worship: Services and Prayers for the Church of England* (London: Archbishops' Council/Church House Publishing, 2000), p. 291.
4 UK Climate Change Committee, 'What Can We All Do?', April 2022, available at: <www.theccc.org.uk/the-need-to-act/what-can-we-all-do/>.
5 Inscription on a church wall in Sussex, *c.* 1730.
6 *Companion to the Standing Orders and Proceedings of the House of Lords*, Appendix K, Prayers for the Parliament; available at: <https://publications.parliament.uk/pa/ld/ldcomp/ldctso58.htm>.

Copyright acknowledgements

The publisher and author acknowledge with thanks permission to reproduce the following. Every effort has been made to seek permission to use copyright material reproduced in this book. The publisher apologizes for those cases where permission might not have been sought and, if notified, will formally seek permission at the earliest opportunity.

Text acknowledgements

Rowan Williams, 'Advent Calendar', from *The Poems of Rowan Williams*, Perpetua/Carcanet Press, 2002, 2014. Reprinted by kind permission of Carcanet Press, Manchester, UK.

Image acknowledgements

Page	Credit
10	The National Gallery, London/akg-images
14	CC by 4.0. Prof. Ed Hawkins (National Centre for Atmospheric Science, University of Reading). <https://showyourstripes.info/s/globe #ShowYourStripes>
32	Tate, Presented by the Contemporary Art Society 1917 © Tate
34	Photograph by NASA on Unsplash
38	Heritage Images/Historica Graphica Collection/akg-images
48	Regents of the University of Michigan, Department of The History of Art, Visual Resources Collections. Michigan-Princeton-Alexandria Expeditions to Mount Sinai
60	© Gerhard Richter 2022 (0130)
64	Tolo Balaguer/Alamy Stock Photo
76	Album/akg-images
86	Royal Academy of Arts, London. Photo John Hammond
92	The National Gallery, London/akg-images
104	The National Gallery, London/akg-images
112	© Pinacoteca di Brera, Milano